DISCOVERED: NOAH'S ARK!

Ronald E. Wyatt
P.O. Box 5931
Madison, TN 37116-5931
© Copyright 1989 Ron Wyatt

Published by World Bible Society
467 Chestnut Street
Nashville, Tennessee 37203

Printed in the United States of America

INTRODUCTION

Many controversies have persisted over the years; some are trivial, and some border on the ridiculous, but some are profound, affecting the very foundations of our beliefs. Those with the most far-reaching and persistent potentials concern the ancient history of mankind as presented in the Holy Bible.

I want to share with you the discovery of Noah's Ark. However, shortly after I became convinced of the authenticity of the Ark, I was divinely guided to several other discoveries which are equally astounding confirmations of the total infallibility of the Bible as Noah's Ark is. These great treasures, preserved by the Hand of God, I believe, are God's great "attention getters" for those who have been discouraged in total belief in the Word of God.

I first became interested in Noah's Ark in 1959 after reading an article in Life Magazine about a "mysterious boat-shaped object" photographed near Mt. Ararat. By 1975, I knew I was going to see this "formation" for myself; I believed it was possibly the remains of Noah's Ark.

In 1960, an expedition from the United States went to examine the object and returned after two days of research at the site with the verdict that it was a natural geological formation. There was nothing of any archaeological interest there.

In 1977, I made the first of 23 (to date) trips to Turkey, and after that first trip, I knew for sure. But gaining the evidence needed to convince the world was another matter.

Today, we have train-loads of evidence. However, it has become a great point of controversy among the ark-hunters. I've been criticized for everything from my methods of research to the fact that I don't speak in tongues. But it's been a small price to pay. I can say without a doubt the Bible is the inspired Word of God and is a historically accurate and reliable guide to the future.

RONALD E. WYATT

DISCOVERED: NOAH'S ARK!

TABLE OF CONTENTS

INTRODUCTION ii

CHAPTER 1 - *THE SEARCH IS OVER!* 1

CHAPTER 2 - *THE YEARS OF RESEARCH*
. . . 1977 - 1987 4

CHAPTER 3 - *SUMMARY OF THE EVIDENCES* 12

CHAPTER 4 - *QUESTIONS I AM MOST FREQUENTLY*
ASKED ABOUT NOAH'S ARK 15

CHAPTER 5 - *ILLUSTRATIONS* 26

CHAPTER 6 - *ONLY THE FIRST OF MANY*
ASTOUNDING DISCOVERIES 31

CHAPTER 7 - *OBSERVATIONS AND REMARKS BY*
CRITICS AND SUPPORTERS (ON
NOAH'S ARK) 37

CHAPTER 8 - *QUOTES AND COMMENTS ON THE*
DISCOVERY OF THE RED SEA
CROSSING SITE AND THE REAL
MT. SINAI 43

CHAPTER 9 - *THE LIVING WORD* 50

CHAPTER 10 - *MY TESTIMONY* 54

CHAPTER 11 - *UNDERSTANDING THE GEOLOGY*
OF THE EARTH AND THE FLOOD 68

CHAPTER 12 - *WHY ARE THESE THINGS BEING*
PRESENTED TO THE WORLD NOW? 84

CONCLUSION 90

CHAPTER 1

THE SEARCH IS OVER!

On June 20, 1987, a group of Turkish government officials and scientists, a film crew from the United States, and an American archaeologist were gathered on a mountain side in the ancient kingdom of Urartu in eastern Turkey. The purpose of this gathering was the dedication of the area as a national park. The area seemed wild and remote; one had the feeling he was thousands of miles from civilization and thousands of years into the past. As shepherds guided their herds through the craggy mountains, the villagers went about their daily lives in stone dwellings reminiscent of a bygone era. The rolling mountains dominated the vast countryside which was broken by towering spires of stone that betrayed the seismic violence that had dominated the region at the dawn of civilization.

Then as one turned and lifted their gaze, the lofty grandeur of the cloud-enshrouded Agri Dagh (Ararat) filled the northern sky. This mystical mountain had for millennia spawned many grandiose and tragic legends of the abodes of the gods and the refuge of the survivors of a world devastated by a universal flood.

As the ceremony began, the guest of honor turned for a moment to gaze upon Agri Dagh's compelling beauty and marvelled as she seemed to pull her veil of clouds about her as a shroud. It was as if the mountain herself knew her deception had been revealed. A tear welled in his eye and found its way down his weathered face as he thought of the countless millions of human kind who had been and were still being swept to destruction by demon-inspired deceptions. These "cunningly devised fables" had been and will be enthusiastically received from lying lips by those "who loved not the truth." Millions had and will continue to pay dearly for "loving and believing a lie." The price:

---

[1] see Rev 22:14 and 15

1

forfeiture of their eternal life.

The dedication of Noah's Ark National Park was festive. The government officials were delighted with the prospects of the influx of tourists and of more money with which to improve the lives of their people. The locals were happy with the good jobs made available through the construction of the new super highway leading to the visitor's center soon to be built overlooking the remains of Noah's Ark. The military officials were happily contemplating their responsibilities of providing safety for the countless visitors. The film crew was happily filming the joyous occasion while thoughts of fame and fortune danced through their minds. Ron Wyatt's silent tears of relief from years of opposition and struggle went unnoticed amid the mirth of the day.

The front page of the Turkish newspaper, *Hurriyet*, dated 21 Harizan 1987 (June 21, 1987):

by Ibrahim Ozturk

NOAH'S ARK AREA IS OPENING TO TOURISM

DOGUBEYAZIT,(hha) - At the Uzengili village, which is near the Dogubeyazit district is located the boat-shaped formation. Scientists from the U.S.A. have confirmed that it is Noah's Ark. The governor has announced that it is now a national park and open for tourists.

At Uzengili village, which is 15 kilometers from Dogubeyazit, Turkish scientists, Mr. Ronald Eldon Wyatt and his team from the U.S.A. made a research of the area. They took samples of the soil. Test results revealed that the soil has iron and fossil boat structures. Scientists confirmed that Noah's Ark is at the Uzengili village.

Mr. Sevket Ekinci, Governor of Agri; Mr. Cengiz Gokce, Head Official of the District of Dogubeyazit; Mr. Osman Baydar, President of the Municipality; some Turkish scientists, and Mr. Wyatt participated in the ceremony opening the area for tourists. Mr. Sevket Ekinci said, "Turkey is a country of great interest for tourists. The Holy Bible and the Koran also say that Noah's Ark is in this area."

Mr. Ekinci added, "It is my pleasure that I am opening this area which is getting great attention for Noah's Ark and I appreciate all the scientists for discovering Noah's Ark. We are laying a foundation for a welcome center for Turkish and foreign tourists. Thank you."

(Translation provided by Mine Uneler, official government liaison provided to work with me during my trips to Turkey. She also acted as my interpreter. This translation was verified in August, 1989 by a Turkish newspaper reporter, who wishes to remain anonymous, working for the "Nashville Tennessean" on an exchange program. Many thanks to them both.)

CHAPTER 2

THE YEARS OF RESEARCH . . . 1977 - 1987

"The night was hot and sultry in eastern Turkey; the heat and darkness seemed like co-conspirators with the danger exploding just outside our door . . .

"Ronnie! Are you awake? We've gotta get outta here! Some of those villagers are trying to kill us!"

My younger son, Ronnie was 15 at the time and had been sleeping in room 303 of the Erzurum Hotel in Dogubeyazit. My other son, Danny, then 17, and I were across the hall in room 308. When we heard the pummeling of heavily-shod feet rushing up the stairs, I shouted commands for the boys to grab what they could and get into the room Ronnie was in, which had a window that opened above the back roof. The window in our room had a fire-escape of sorts, and we'd be sitting ducks if we stayed in there.

We grabbed what we could and barricaded ourselves in room 303 by shoving the bed against the door and pushing the chest between the bed and the wall. Little was spoken as our minds raced, trying to comprehend what was happening to us. We could hear the attempted use of a pass-key in the lock as the door appeared to strain against the weight of the angry mob just outside, threatening to disintegrate and loose upon us the furious knot of assailants. Our mouths and throats were excruciatingly dry from the lack of safe drinking water and also from the rush of adrenaline propelled into our systems. Desperately, our minds cast about for any means of escape, and I wondered how my well-laid plans had deteriorated to this . . ."

That scenario took place during my first trip to Turkey in 1977. And it was that trip which provided me with the discoveries that proved to me the boat-shaped object I was in search of was indeed the remains of Noah's Ark. It would be another ten years of painstaking and costly research before the Turkish government was convinced the boat was real, but today the evidence is in, and soon the entire world will be able to see the Ark remains for itself. The multi-million dollar highway is near completion; this will provide visitors easy access to the site and the modern, spacious visitor's center above the Ark.

DETAILS OF THE SEARCH

During the summer of 1977, my two sons and I found ourselves at risk in a strange country amongst a people of strange speech. They attempted to rob and possibly kill us. (For the record, the same thing could and often does happen to tourists from other countries who visit our country and fall among the criminal element of our society.) This "nervousing experience", (a term coined by my youngest son, Ronnie, that fit the situation quite accurately), was the beginning of many years of slow, meticulous, frustrating research that culminated in undeniable proof of the reality and location of the remains of Noah's Ark.

Our first trip to eastern Turkey produced a veritable landslide of discoveries and excitement and set the pace for a breathtakingly rapid sequence of discoveries that left us in a state of mind that had us mentally "pinching ourselves" from the difficulty of accepting the reality of it all!

Our discoveries on the 1977 trip included several massive, pierced anchor stones that bore an eight-cross iconographic representation of the eight survivors of the flood. These crosses were inscribed by the Byzantine and Crusader Christians, which proved that something or someone convinced them that these pierced stones were relics from the Ark of Noah. One of the stones bore the inscription of Nimrod, the builder of the tower of Babel and several great cities of early antiquity. These symbols of Nimrod were crosses with the outline of a boat (the Ark?) attached to the base of the cross. This symbolized

5

his claim that he had preserved mankind in the face of their attempted destruction by the gods. The boat at the foot of the cross represented the means he claimed to have used to save mankind. The horizontal member of the cross represented heaven, and the vertical member of the cross represented the tower of Babel, which was the pathway to heaven he had promised his followers he would provide. After Nimrod's death, the boat symbol was placed at the top of the vertical member of the cross and is the symbol of life in the Egyptian hieroglyphics and the symbol of Nimrod's (Osirus) presence in heaven from whence he cares for his earthly followers.

We found two grave markers that bore the eight-cross symbols of Noah and his family above an ancient, petroglyphic portrayal of Noah's death on one marker and that of his wife on the other. These grave markers were in the front of a very ancient stone house. These markers and the house have been vandalized, and over one hundred million U.S. dollars worth of gold and gemstones were stolen from the graves. The Turkish authorities are seeking to recover these precious artifacts and to punish the thieves. At present, they are aware of the identity of the most probable person responsible for this outrage. He is a man who has been involved in the Ark search in the past, but he dropped from the public eye shortly after the theft from Noah's and his wife's graves.

We located and photographed several other inscriptions and physical remains of the flood and the Ark. We got a brief look at the boat remains before we were forced to flee for our lives. Upon our arrival back in the states, we had our super-eight movie film developed and were delighted to see that we had good photographic documentation of all the artifacts and inscriptions.

Shortly after our return, a friend called to inform me that an M.D. PhD (Dr. Bill Shea) from a university in Michigan had written several articles that stated his belief that the boat formation was related to the landing site of

Noah's Ark. I contacted Dr. Bill Shea and shared our discoveries with him. He was delighted, reviewed the inscriptions, recognized the pierced stone anchors as probable relics from the Ark, and joined with me in applying to the Turkish government for permission to excavate the boat-shaped formation. The Turkish authorities declined to give us a permit at that time. We got the same reply after a second request. We were stymied.

My sons and I spent the summer of 1978 locating and documenting the site where Moses and the Habiru (Hebrew slaves, which included many of the descendants of Abraham by his three wives; Sarah, Hagar, and Keturah; these women are the fore-mothers of all the Arab and Jewish peoples) crossed the Red Sea.

Yet, all the while, we were unable to forget the fantastic discoveries associated with Noah's Ark. We, with some trusted friends, prayed that God would see fit to send an earthquake that would in some manner expose the boat formation for what it was without injury to any of the inhabitants of the area. Watching the evening news on the 28th of December, 1978, I was thrilled to see that an earthquake had hit the area where the Ark remains were located and that there had been no casualties! I made arrangements to return to the site, and arrived there in the early summer of 1979. The formation had been split down the middle along its entire length, and the earth had fallen away from its sides. This allowed me to take clean, fresh samples from five locations along the center and sides of the boat. It also made it possible to carefully measure the depth of the object along its length, and to document the dimensions of several of the main structural timbers that were exposed. I photographed the formation and its exposed structures and returned home with a veritable treasure trove of archaeological data and specimens!

Galbraith Laboratories of Knoxville, Tennessee was highly recommended, and it was to them I entrusted the care and analysis of these precious samples. The results were astounding! The raw carbon[2] content showed the object to be composed of decayed wood, and a high concentration of oxidized metal was shown. We had taken three samples from the site at distances that guaranteed them to be out of the geological influence of the boat remains. These compared favorably with chemical values of normal countryside and proved that the boat formation was composed of decayed and oxidized archaeological remains!

I shared this data with Bill Shea, and on the strength of this evidence, we made reapplication to the Turkish authorities and were again put off. Dr. Shea and I decided that the high metallic contents of the formation warranted evaluation (investigation) with metal detection devices. We contacted Whites Electronic Corporation of Sweet Home, Oregon and were supplied with their best-quality metal detection equipment. This was done during the interval between 1979 and 1984.

Again, my sons and I were working in the Middle East, documenting the methods used by the ancient Egyptians to build the pyramids. During the fall of 1983 I became aware that Colonel James Irwin of High Flight Foundation, located in Colorado Springs, Colorado, was searching for the remains of Noah's Ark. I contacted him by phone and was invited to visit him and to share the details of our research with him. He was "intrigued" by our research and wanted to see the boat formation and possibly work with us on the investigation and documentation of the Red Sea crossing site, pyramid building, and the Ark of the Covenant. He, Mary, (his wife), and their family are wonderful friends, and we have highly valued their friendship. It was Colonel Irwin, I believe, who helped get my sons and me out of prison in Saudi Arabia, where we had been mistakenly accused of being Israeli spies! The details of the discovery of the real Mt. Sinai include the altar, the twelve pillars of stone (22x18 ft. double-walled towers of stone), plus the remains

---

[2] See copies of these first 2 lab reports in the chapter "Illustrations"

of a twelve columned, white marbled shrine, dedicated to the "Mountain Of God" (Yahweh) and twelve petroglyphs of Hathor and Apis, the cow and bull gods of Egypt (the golden calf).

In August, 1984, accompanied by Colonel Jim Irwin and armed with the deep probe metal detectors courteously provided by Whites Electronics, we returned to the boat formation. (Another well-known electronics firm promised us some metal detection equipment, but to date we haven't received it.) In the company of Colonel Irwin, Marvin Steffins, Bulant Atalay, "Whatcha" McCullum, a military escort and a Turkish army officer, Orhan Basar, I demonstrated a pattern of metals and/or their oxides that showed the outline of a boat in the formation. The army officer, under my direction, took several small samples from metal brackets and petrified timbers.

Mr. Steffins called a news conference a few days later, displayed some bags of specimens "from Noah's Ark", and claimed the discovery. This triggered an international "incident" that resulted in my being accused of stealing archaeological treasures from Turkey by Ted Koppel on A.B.C.'s NIGHTLINE, the night of August 27, 1984! A call to the Turkish mission at the U.N. led to my exoneration by the MINISTER OF CULTURE AND TOURISM, MUKERREM TASCIOGLU, in an A.P. interview on August 30, 1984. When the "incident" blew over, we proceeded with the analysis of the samples per agreement with the Turkish authorities. The results of these analyses confirmed those taken in 1979 and proved that the formation contained a massive, ancient boat that was built of massive, wooden timbers held in place by many massive, metal brackets and spikes!

From the data accumulated from 1977-1984 I was able to construct a scale model of Noah's Ark. In fact, we built several models, presenting one to the governor of Agri providence, The Honorable SEVKET EKINCI, and another of the models is stored in Ankara for presentation to PRESIDENT KENNAN EVEREN when the opportunity arises.

In the winter of 1985 I received calls from DAVID FASOLD, a specialist in old boat research and identification, and JOHN BAUMGARDNER, PhD., a geophysicist from Las Alamos National Laboratories. I invited them to accompany me to the site later in the year. David introduced the Molecular Frequency Generator into the research, and along with the equipment from Whites Electronics, it identified the massive structure of a boat enclosed within the boat formation!

During July and August of 1985, with financial assistance arranged by Dr. Baumgardner and accompanied by David Fasold, John Baumgardner, Tom Anderson, Maylon Wilson, Tom Thaxton, Tom Jarriel, Jim Burroughs, Niel Richline, George House, Judith Moses (ABC's 20/20 producer) and others, (those included on my permit from the Turkish government were: David Fasold, John Baumgardner, Normajean Baumgardner, Thomas Anderson, Todd Fisher, Scott Snider, William Shea, Fredrich Bach, Klaus Wattenbach, Zafer Akcay) we planned to scan the formation with a SUBSURFACE INTERFACE RADAR SYSTEM. This system was developed by GEOPHYSICAL SURVEYS SYSTEMS INC. of Hudson, New Hampshire and was accompanied by their geologist, Tom Fenner. The preliminary survey and lay-out of the site progressed smoothly. We were accompanied by a group of 30 Turkish Commandos, who hid in the surrounding countryside for our protection. Turkish intelligence had informed me that an attempt would likely be made to kidnap or kill Colonel Irwin and/or myself. The attempt made by some **Iranian terrorists resulted in the deaths of five terrorists and three Turkish soldiers!** Martial law was declared in the area, our plans were trashed, and the radar scan waited until later that fall.

We surveyed the site with three types of metal detectors

and two subsurface radar systems. Their data, along with core drilling samples, proved beyond any doubt that a VERY LARGE, (515 FEET) VERY ANCIENT BOAT (IDENTIFIED BY INSCRIPTIONS AS NOAH'S ARK) LIES WITHIN THE BOAT FORMATION!

CHAPTER 3

A SUMMARY OF THE EVIDENCES

The Turkish government has meticulously observed and kept records of the activities and claims of all who have "looked for Noah's Ark" over the last 50 years. They followed our research (by our invitation) and STEP BY SCIENTIFIC STEP became convinced of the reality of the remains of NUH'UN GEMISI (Noah's Ark) buried within the boat formation.

The reasons which convinced the Turkish government and POSITIVELY IDENTIFY THE REMAINS OF THE LARGE ANCIENT BOAT WITHIN THE BOAT FORMATION AS THOSE OF NOAH'S ARK are as follows:

1. The formation was positively identified as a boat by a number of skilled photogrammetry experts from a set of aerial photographs. In a quote from Rene Noorbergen's book "The Ark File", Dr. Arthur Brandenburger, professor of photogrammetry at Ohio State in Columbus, Ohio, stated after careful study of the photo of the site, "I have no doubt at all that this object is a ship. In my entire career I have never seen an object like this on a stereo photo."

Dr. Brandenburger went on the 1960 expedition to the site, and after the team returned home with the verdict that there was nothing there of any archaeological interest, Dr. Brandenburger was still not convinced. In further quotes from the above book, he says later, "Our measurements in the field verify our laboratory findings. In my opinion further study of this peculiar symmetrical phenomenon should be made by an expert in tectonics."

"Meanwhile, I have received my developed colored slides of the ship-shaped formation, and I still must say it is an amazing feature. It is doubtless a mystery, and I come always more to the conclusion that our official statement to the press was too negative. The interpretation of the formation is of utmost difficulty, and I am not anymore so sure that, from a serious scientific standpoint, a sole surface archaeological investigation of only two days entitles us to state that the formation is not the ark."

Dr. Brandenburger was exactly right.

2. Twelve years of electronic and mechanical probing has positively identified it as a boat. See Figure 1 for the results from the metal detection surveys and the radar scans.

3. Repeated chemical analysis of many different samples, taken at different times by different people and analyzed at different laboratories, positively prove it to be composed of very ancient wood and metal. See Figure 2 for comparison testing on samples by Galbraith Labs in Knoxville, Tennessee.

4. Samples of petrified wood have been located and taken from the structure in the presence of many witnesses. In addition to previous tests, I have additional samples which have metal brackets and rust, which were videoed as they were retrieved from the boat. I will have them tested at various testing facilities in the future and in the presence of witnesses.

5. A large number of ancient and medieval inscriptions near the site positively identify it as Noah's Ark. There will be more on these inscriptions in our later book, which will include photographs.

6. Its 515 foot length, its 138 foot width (splayed) are the measurements of Noah's Ark as recorded by Moses (educated to use the ancient Egyptian cubit) in the Book of Genesis. See an explanation under "Questions I am Most Frequently Asked about Noah's Ark".

7. It is located in the mountains of Urartu (Ararat) as specified in the Bible.

8. Its location at an elevation of 6300 feet above sea level is above any possible height reachable by a "local flood" but is below the maximum water level that would result

from all the water of our planet washing the earth's surface (7000-8000 feet).

9. Its location, many miles from any present or ancient body of water that would support it, defies any other explanation.

10. Its massive size and weight make it impossible that it could have been "trundled" (dragged) this distance from water, and its altitude above present and past sea levels defies any other explanation.

11. Contrary to a touched up photograph, which has been widely circulated, it's the only formation of its kind on planet earth, other than remains of other ancient boats of much smaller size.

12. Your writer, in the presence of Turkish authorities and other observers, performed an electronic survey of a site that some of our critics said resembled the boat formation (the similarities were vague at best, nonexistent in actuality); the metal detectors and sub-surface radar scans showed nothing in the site that were not present anywhere in the area.

13. A careful electronic survey of the area around the formation showed none of the structures present in the formation.

14. Chemical analysis of the area around the formation showed only normal traces of the metallic oxides and organic carbon which are present in large amounts in the formation.

15. Train loads of petrified wood are present in the formation, but there is little to be found in the rest of eastern Turkey.

16. Many ancient historians record that the remains of Noah's Ark were to be visited in this area.

CHAPTER 4

QUESTIONS I AM MOST FREQUENTLY ASKED ABOUT NOAH'S ARK

1) The "object" you claim is the remains of Noah's Ark is about 515 feet long and 138 feet wide. The Bible says the Ark was 300 cubits long and 50 cubits wide. I always believed that would mean the Ark would have been 450 feet long by 75 feet wide. How do you explain this discrepancy with the Bible?

Answer: This is one of the most exciting confirmations of the authenticity of the object being the Ark, in my estimation! The Bible tells us how Noah's offspring eventually migrated to what became Babylon, then at the confusion of languages, Ham's descendants migrated to what became Egypt. The Encyclopedia Britannica (1985 edition) states:

> *"Although there is evidence that many early civilizations devised standards of measurements and some tools for measuring, the Egyptian cubit is generally recognized as having been the most ubiquitous standard of linear measurement in the very ancient world."*

The royal Egyptian cubit was 20.62 inches. Now, if we consider the Biblical statement that Moses was "learned in all the wisdom of Egypt" - Acts 7:22, as the author of Genesis, he would have been referring to the only cubit he knew. 300 cubits = 515.5 feet. 50 cubits = 85.9 feet. The measurement of the length of the boat, taken in August, 1985 by Maylon Wilson and Baumgardner of Los Alamos Laboratory with sophisticated measurement devices, showed the inside length of the boat to be 515.7 feet! David Fasold's measurement of the same was exactly 515 feet!

The width of 138 feet, (my measurement and also David's) may at first seem to present a problem until we consider it carefully. The boat is splayed. The height given in the Bible is 30 cubits or 51.55 feet. The width is given as 50 cubits or 85.916 feet. The total of both sides plus the width is 189.016 feet - far too wide. But if the hull of the ship was exactly half the entire height of the boat, and the hull splayed outward, the width would be 137.466 feet! Our later metal detection results confirmed these figures as well as the sub-surface interface radar scans.

2) I understand that other creationists have stated that what you claim to be petrified wood extending from the formation cannot possibly be wood. Isn't it a simple matter to prove something is petrified wood?

Answer: Yes it is, normally. Let me refer you to the section on "The Geology of the Earth" for an explanation on the petrification process. However, part of the identification of a petrified object is visual. If it looks like a shell, chances are it's a shell. If it looks like wood, then it's wood. But there's a problem with this wood - it looks like wood except for one thing; it has no growth rings. Now, if we truly believe the Biblical description of the earth before the flood, we <u>know</u> that there couldn't possibly be any growth rings in pre-flood wood[3]. In "The New Larousse Encyclopedia of the Earth", page 369, we read:

> *"To support trunks of six-foot base diameter and 60- to 100- foot height, tissues must have increased in thickness from year to year. There was, as we have already said, secondary bark and wood, similar to that of modern trees but lacking the spring and winter rings which correspond to seasonal alternation of moisture and dryness."*

---

[3] See the last paragraph under "The Flood" in Chapter 11 on growth rings and pre-flood geology. See also Gen. 2:6.

This is in reference to ancient sigillarias found without any growth rings. But isn't it a pity that I had to go to a book that refers to the earth's age in "millions of years" to find a reference corroborating the fact that these fossils have been found *without growth rings*? If growth rings were in the wood of the Ark, it would be a fake or replica.

3) What about laboratory testing of samples from the Ark; have you had this done?

Answer: Yes I obtained samples from the boat itself and from the land around the Ark. I had several of these samples tested at Galbraith Labs in Knoxville, Tennessee. Just like medical tests, these results have to be read and interpreted by people trained to do so, so I will quote William Shea, M.D. PhD., Professor of Archaeology and History of Antiquity, in his report to the Turkish government dated February 20, 1987:

"The formation was struck by an earthquake in December of 1978. As a result it was cracked lengthwise and partially split open. This opening made it possible for Wyatt to obtain relatively fresh internal soil samples from it when he returned to the site in September of 1979. In a test run on this sample, along with another sample taken from the field outside of the formation, the organic carbon content was measured. The soil from the formation tested at 4.95% while the soil from the field around the formation tested at 1.88%. This degree of difference is consistent with the prior presence of some organic matter (like wood) in the formation."

Since then, I have had numerous other specimens tested with similar results, which I will publish at a later date. Also, these tests revealed extremely high metallic contents, which caused me to wonder if there might not be metal in the Ark itself. This led to the future metal detection testing which revealed the fantastic structure of a massive boat.

4) Explain the metal detection tests and how it could prove any internal structure. Couldn't it just be trace metal in the soil?

Answer: No. On the Ark, the metal detecting equipment gave positive readings on its calibrated dial and by sound at numerous points all over the boat. We were able to determine that there was significant amounts of metal present and that it appeared to be in a pattern. The testing of the surrounding area was completely negative. In May of 1985, John Baumgardner and David Fasold, a marine salvor from Florida, accompanied me to the site, and with the metal detectors and David's new type of metal detector, a molecular frequency generator, we mapped out the metal readings with plastic tapes. It revealed a distinct linear subsurface pattern. We repeated this again in August of 1985, with John Baumgardner and myself accompanied this time by Maylon Wilson, also of Los Alamos Laboratories, and Tom Anderson, a lawyer from Indio, California, who filmed the entire event. We videoed the tests ourselves on both occasions and photographed it thoroughly.

On the outer wall of the boat, striations appears which are keenly visible along the east side of the upper portion and the west side of the lower portion. On the striations, the metal readings were positive while the spaces between were totally negative.

5) What about the radar scans you mention? What exactly is sub-surface interface radar, and what did the use of it prove?

Answer: Without getting highly technical, this type of radar works by the generation of an electromagnetic pulse which is radiated into the earth from a broad band width antenna. This pulse can be focused to a particular depth where it is then reflected back and recorded on a graphic recorder similar to an EKG. Quite a sophisticated device, it requires training to operate and to read the results accurately. I received thorough training at Geophysical Survey Systems, Inc. in Hudson, New Hampshire. The first scan took place in July of 1986. On this expedition were myself, Baumgardner and Anderson from the August, 1985 expedition, as well as Mrs. Baumgardner, Dr. William Shea of Andrews University and two cameramen, Todd Fisher and Scott Snider, from Los Angeles. This radar scan confirmed, with astounding detail, the same pattern demonstrated by the metal detectors. Where it was remotely possible to have incorrectly connected the lines resulting from the metal detectors, the radar scan <u>showed</u> what can only be identified as a keel, keelsons and bulkheads from a boat of tremendous size.

6) What do the scientists and other experts you have taken to the "boat" say; do <u>they</u> believe it is the Ark?

Answer: One who is totally convinced is David Fasold. David has written a book entitled "The Ark of Noah" which details much of our research, and while we disagree on some matters I don't feel are significant or cause for doubt as to the identity of the boat, I highly recommend it. He is meticulously thorough in his research and recording of the data. I must give David a great deal of credit in the research and wish to add he was the most enjoyable person I have ever worked with. He knew the first time he laid eyes on it that it was a boat. And he's an expert in shipwrecks.

Dr. William Shea has worked with me on this from the very beginning. He is a professional in the field of archaeology and ancient history and most open-minded to facts. While I have not a statement from him recently, I will quote from an article he wrote for "Archaeology and Biblical Research", Winter, 1988, entitled "Noah's Ark?" on page 14:

". . . The last half of the list point to the general conclusion that the remains of a ship appear to be present in this formation. The first half are of a more specific nature that would connect the remains of such a ship with the Ark of Noah described in Genesis. The progressive convergence of these various lines of evidence seem to confirm the conclusion that some of the remains of Noah's Ark lie within this unusual formation."

Dr. John Baumgardner appears to have changed his mind about what he believes. So as to avoid misquoting him I will quote from David's book, "The Ark of Noah":

"John didn't hear the remark. I think he was off someplace in Tubal-cain's foundry five thousand years ago. He held in his hand a piece of wrought iron. The grain of the stretched and hammered angle bracket still clearly visible.

It was complete pandemonium after that. Once John knew what to look for, fittings were all over the place. He could walk down the top of the wall with the detector going beep,...beep every two or three steps. Now it was the trained eye of a scientist, looking for things out of place in the natural covering of the mud, followed by his 'Look at this!' growing in excitement. I kept the video going as I ran around, stumbling behind him, then moved to the mound to record his discoveries from a distance to give perspective to the viewer. No sooner had I left him when he suddenly yelled, 'Undecomposed iron!'

I ran down the mound again and crouched to my knees. I zoomed in on the mud wall. There, surrounded by the brown matrix of mud, was a perfectly rectangular beam end of a bluish-gray agglomeration of small rough stones. The upper and lower right corners were absolutely square, and projecting from within were what appeared to be iron flakes which had given the signals."

The results of the analysis on that metal bracket are recorded also in David's book:

"I hurriedly opened the first-class envelope labeled 'Los Alamos National Laboratory.' It contained the semiquantitative analysis of the iron samples we had recovered from the Ark. The stoichiometric results were impressive, with the seven running from 60 percent through 91.84 percent FE203. The highest reading was obtained from an angular bracket."

Later we read of a news broadcast which David meticulously recorded:

"Soon there followed daily broadcasts: '. . . has this report on what the scientists have found so far . . . could this be the final resting place of Noah's Ark? . . . Dr. John Baumgardner, a geophysicist at the Los Alamos Research Lab in New Mexico . . . using a metal detector, Baumgardner has been able to confirm the existence of metal at regular intervals. Baumgardner says he believes that metal is at the points where these lines intersect, giving rise to speculation metal was used in the infrastructure of the craft.' "

Finally, when our local newspaper here in Nashville did a story on the Ark on August 16, 1989, I gave them his name and told them to call him. From "The Tennessean":

"A former Wyatt colleague, geophysicist John Baumgardner of the Los Alamos National Laboratory in Los Alamos, N.M. said the intriguing hieroglyphics and high levels of iron oxides found there are 'very encouraging', but the evidence is still too meager to make any conclusions."

"The amazingly symmetrical shape of the site can be explained by the flow of mudslides in the area over *time."*

But my favorite "critic" of not only the site but myself, was also contacted at my request and quoted in the same article:

> " *'As much as I want to believe it, I have to say the formation is rock from top to bottom, and anyone knowledgeable who steps onto it knows that,' said John Morris, head of the Creation Science Institute in San Diego.*
>
> *'The main problem with Wyatt is he's too free with his conclusions and hasn't submitted his data to independent researchers. He's not a geologist.' "*

7) I don't see how these anchor stones prove it's the Ark. If they are several miles from the site you claim is the Ark, how does that prove anything?

Answer: The anchor stones have tremendous significance in more ways than one. First of all, they are by far the largest anchor stones ever found in the history of the world. The leading authority on anchor stones is considered to be Honor Frost, who in 1973 published, "Ancore, the Potsherd of Marine Archaeology: On the Recording of Pierced Stones from the Mediterranean". Based on her thorough research, we learn that 700 kgs., or 1,543 lbs. is one of the heaviest, if not the heaviest, anchor stone ever found. That is until these. One of the largest I've found is almost 11 feet tall, but the average height is 10 feet by a 5 foot width. David Fasold, in his book, estimates the average weight of these   anchor stones to be 8,700 lbs.

To date, there are 10 of these that I have seen. There are several more that I believe to be anchors, but they are partially buried in an upright position and exhibit some of the same characteristics as those we are sure of. Eight of them have the inscriptions which make it evident that some people at some point in time made a direct connection between these and Noah and the Ark. However, some people suggest that whoever carved the crosses probably carved the anchor stones. I know this is definitely not the case, as when I was at the site in April, I found two more anchor stones which were buried and just barely surfacing for obviously the first time and these did not have any crosses or any other carvings on them!

As for the placement of these anchor stones, it becomes quite evident that as the Ark drifted between two submerged peaks in a ridge of small mountains, the first two anchors snagged and tethered the boat until Noah removed the covering and saw the tops of the mountains. We found a large piece of petrified bark in the same vicinity which I believe to be a portion of that covering. He then cut them loose, leaving them on the two peaks, a short distance apart. As the boat made a direct line through these mountains toward its final resting place, seven more anchors, and probably more, were cut loose and landed near, if not exactly, where they are at present. The village where five of these are located is in a direct line with the twin peaks of the ridge where the first two dropped. The two that are buried are also in this direct line, and finally about eight miles further, about 1/4 mile below the boat, lies the 10th one.

These anchor stones are far too large to be carried by men. It has been suggested that they aren't anchors at all and that the holes are the means by which they were dragged to their present locations. This is impossible, as the location and size of the holes are such that out of water they would break right off under the tremendous stress. Only in the buoyancy of the water could they be held by ropes. Of interest also is the fact that the holes have a larger inner diameter than outer; when the ropes were secured through the holes, knots were tied inside the "scooped-out" hole, and as the water swelled the knotted rope, it was prevented from rubbing and eventually wearing the rope in two from the friction.

8) If the Turkish government has really agreed with your finding and declared that this is really the Ark, why hasn't the whole world heard about it? Why are the other ark searches still going on?

Answer: As you read at the beginning of this book, they announced it in their own newspapers. But before they publicized a fact such as this on a world wide scale, they built a visitor's center and are still working on what is at least a six- and possibly eight-lane highway which leads to the site. This is a remote area. There isn't any quick and easy way to get there from Erzurum; you have to go by "taksi" or bus for at least a good four to five hours. While there are a few hotels in the area, there are certainly not enough for a sudden and tremendous influx of tourists. The Turkish government will make the announcement as soon as they are ready. The biggest problem they are facing at the present is the theft of great archaeological treasures from this area. I mentioned the theft of Noah's wife's grave; I was contacted directly to see if I had any knowledge of who could have done such a thing and was told that one piece of jewelry had sold on the black-market in Istanbul for $75,000,000.00! Of course, it had to be quite an incredible piece, and the description of it alone was more than a person could comprehend. The locals have discovered that tourists will buy anything with a cross inscribed on it, so they are breaking some of the artifacts up and selling them.

Then, they must consider the Ark itself. At present, there is no protection for it. People could begin breaking off pieces for souvenirs and destroy it very quickly in the delicate condition it is presently in. They do have a caretaker who has wild dogs guarding it now, but it could be a potentially destructive situation to encourage too much tourism at present. On my last visit in August of this year, I noticed they had even taken down the "Nuh'un Gemisi" sign which greeted visitors at the foot of the road leading to it. However, on the Sunday after Thanksgiving, 1988, Connie Chung mentioned on her brief "news break" that the Turkish government was going to make the announcement sometime next year, meaning 1989, I presumed.

CHAPTER 5

ILLUSTRATIONS

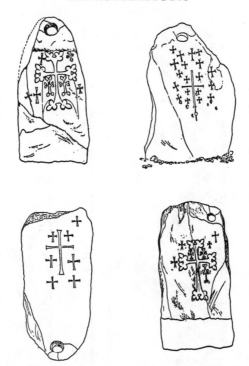

The anchor stones represented above are #2, #3, #4, and #5 that I found. The crosses are of the Byzantine and Crusader (Maltese) design, which is evidence that these peoples recognized these pierced anchor stones as relics of Noah's Ark. The eight-cross iconograph represents Noah, his wife, his three sons and their three wives - the sole human survivors of the flood.

An average of about 10 feet in height and 5 feet in width, the average weight, out of water, would be about 8,700 lbs.! Far too heavy to have been carried up to the mountain peaks they were found resting on, there can be no other explanation than the fact that they today lie near the same spot as when they were released from the Ark.

CROSS-SECTION OF RECONSTRUCTED FRONT END OF ARK SUPERIMPOSED UPON THE PRESENT REMAINS

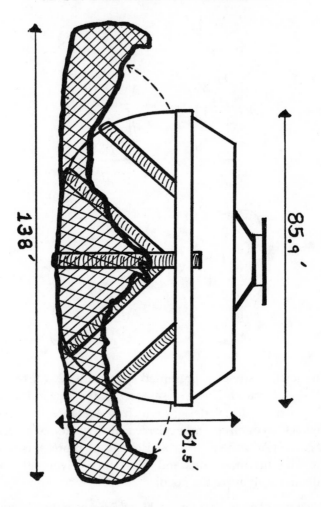

Note the presence of five keels. Similar structures are not found in any other ancient boats. Sub-surface interface radar confirmed visible evidence of these keels. The Ark's design was exceptional for it's hydrodynamics and durability.

MAIN BULKHEADS ON THE FIRST DECK-LEVEL OF THE ARK AS REVEALED BY SUB-SURFACE INTERFACE RADAR SCANNING

SUB-SURFACE INTERFACE RADAR SCAN RESULTS

1 2 3 4 5 6 7 8 9 10

47' 40.5 29.5 20' 31' 46' 30' 128' 43' 100'

N

Length of bulkhead, if able to determine a close measurement: 1. - 35'; 2. - 63'; 4. - 86'; 8. - 56' each side to center area of 20' width for total of 138'; 10. - 51'.

Total inside length - 515 feet.

Width (splayed) at widest section - 138 feet.

28

LABORATORY RESULTS ON FIRST SAMPLES TAKEN FROM THE ARK AND AREA OUTSIDE AS CONTROL SAMPLE

P. O. BOX 4187, 2323 SYCAMORE DR., KNOXVILLE, TENNESSEE 37921 / 615 546-1335

CERTIFICATE OF ANALYSIS

Mr. Ronald E. Wyatt
C.P.O. Box 931
Madison, Tennessee 37115

October 9, 1979

Received: Oct. 1st

Your Sample No. ___1___   Our No. I-3967 ___ gave the following results:

Ultimate Analysis,	As Received,	Dry Basis,	Mineral Analysis,	Ignited Basis,
% Moisture			% Phos. pentoxide, P_2O_5	0.28
% Carbon			% Silica, SiO_2	51.29
% Hydrogen			% Ferric Oxide, Fe_2O_3	9.71
% Nitrogen			% Alumina, Al_2O_3	15.27
% Chlorine			% Titania, TiO_2	1.33
% Sulfur			% Lime, CaO	9.35
% Ash			% Magnesia, MgO	3.94
% Oxygen (by diff.)			% Sulfur Trioxide, SO_3	0.37
			% Potassium Oxide, K_2O	2.30
Proximate Analysis,	As Received,	Dry Basis,	% Sodium Oxide, Na_2O	2.43
			% Undetermined	

	As Received	Dry Basis,
% Moisture		
% Ash		
% Volatile Matter		
% Fixed Carbon	BTU/lb.	

Sulfur Forms,	As Received,	Dry Basis,	% Carbon	1.88
% Pyritic Sulfur				
% Sulfate Sulfur				
% Organic Sulfur				
% Total Sulfur				

Note difference in carbon content. The significantly higher level indicates decayed organic material in a high concentration, such as a wooden structure.

LABORATORY RESULTS ON FIRST SAMPLES TAKEN FROM THE ARK AND AREA OUTSIDE AS CONTROL SAMPLE

P. O. BOX 4187, 2323 SYCAMORE DR., KNOXVILLE, TENNESSEE 37921 / 615 546-1335

CERTIFICATE OF ANALYSIS

Mr. Ronald E. Wyatt
Page 2
October 9, 1979

Your Sample No. __2__ Our No. __I-3968__ gave the following results:

Ultimate Analysis,	As Received,	Dry Basis,	Mineral Analysis,	Ignited Basis,
% Moisture			% Phos. pentoxide, P_2O_5	0.23
% Carbon			% Silica, SiO_2	48.02
% Hydrogen			% Ferric Oxide, Fe_2O_3	6.56
% Nitrogen			% Alumina, Al_2O_3	14.01
% Chlorine			% Titania, TiO_2	0.44
% Sulfur			% Lime, CaO	17.41
% Ash			% Magnesia, MgO	3.02
% Oxygen (by diff.)			% Sulfur Trioxide, SO_3	0.17
			% Potassium Oxide, K_2O	3.09
Proximate Analysis,	As Received,	Dry Basis,	% Sodium Oxide, Na_2O	0.94
			% Undetermined	

Proximate Analysis,	As Received,	Dry Basis,
% Moisture		
% Ash		As Received / Dry Basis,
% Volatile Matter		
% Fixed Carbon		BTU/lb.

Sulfur Forms,	As Received,	Dry Basis,
% Pyritic Sulfur		% Carbon 4.95
% Sulfate Sulfur		
% Organic Sulfur		
% Total Sulfur		

Gail R. Hutchens Gail R. Hutchens, Exec. Vice-President

Note difference in carbon content. The significantly higher level indicates decayed organic material in a high concentration, such as a wooden structure.

PRINTOUT OF LATERAL SUB-SURFACE INTERFACE RADAR SCAN SHOWING INTERNAL STRUCTURES

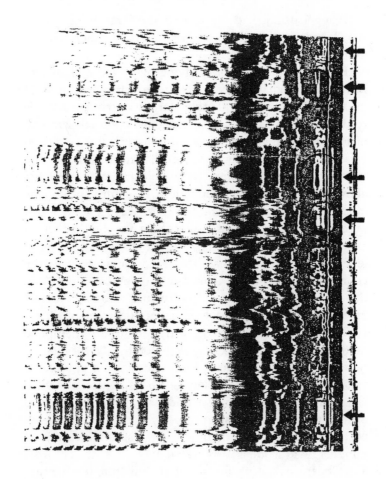

Note line of rectangular shaped structures representing deck timbers. The more rectangular ones have been better preserved than the more irregular patterns.

CHAPTER 6

ONLY THE FIRST OF MANY ASTOUNDING DISCOVERIES!

When I decided to try to find the remains of Noah's Ark, I had no thought of discovering any other artifacts from the past.

However, the years of studying every piece of ancient history and archaeologically-related research had brought me to the brink of several other startling discoveries. While reading Herodotus' histories, I happened upon a description of how the pyramids were built. "The method employed was to build it in steps, or, as some call them, tiers or terraces. When the base was complete, the blocks for the first tier above it were lifted from ground level by contrivances made of short timbers; on this first tier there was another, which raised the blocks a stage higher, then yet another which raised them higher still. Each tier, or story, had its set of levers." This comment has been read for many years by countless people; more than a few times by myself, but due to its nonspecific term "contrivance", no one pursued an understanding of this method of construction. While reviewing ancient Egyptian inscriptions in an attempt to better understand the chronology of the "dynasties", I noticed that the glyph used to indicate the act of building was an abbreviated set of levers! I began sketching these levers and their mirror image. Suddenly, the whole process of pyramid building flashed into my mind! The simplicity of the machines and methods was astounding! Within minutes I had made a working model from strips cut from a cardboard box. With the aid of my children, brother and friends we soon made several working models of the machines.

In the fall of 1978, an international trade fair was held in Nashville, Tennessee. An Egyptian business friend that had charge of the Egyptian display asked my sons and I if we would set up a working demonstration of our pyramid building machines. The story was in the local news and on T.V. It also ran in an A.P. release. Archaeologists, Egyptologists, ancient history buffs, and hundreds of other inquisitive people flocked to our demonstration. They came with towering and freely verbalized skepticism. After watching the demonstration, they stood agape, shook their heads and expressed dismay that such a simple solution to so long time a mystery had not been solved ages ago!

In the early spring of 1979 my children (Michelle, Daniel, and Ronnie) and I took several working models of the machines to Egypt. We are grateful to Royal Jordanian Airlines for their kindness in flying all those timbers to Egypt at no cost to us! We contacted Nassef Mohamed Hassan who was the director of Antiquities for Egypt and a man we had given diagrams showing the pyramid building process in the fall of 1978. He was delighted to give us permission to set the machines up on the middle pyramid at Giza (Chephren). We demonstrated the building technique on the actual pyramid, allowed a news crew from Nippon T.V. to film a brief clip, and filmed the process for our film library. Mr. Hassan and I were invited to explain the discovery and technique on a Voice of America radio broadcast! The entire process with diagrams will be published in our forthcoming book DISCOVERED: HOW? & WHO? - THE PYRAMIDS.

As the results of years of fascinating research into the history of ancient Egypt, I was able to discover the location of ancient Succoth, which the Bible says is the starting point of the Exodus led by Moses. The Bible states that the slaves "encamped" (meaning that they first entered the camping mode) at Succoth. It then says that they took the southern route to Horeb to avoid military conflict with the Philistines. There was but one southern route to ancient Midian. It was through a trail of canyons (wadis) that crossed the modern Sinai Peninsula to the west side of the coastal mountain range that parallels the west shore of the Gulf of Aqaba.

It turned north at this point and went to the northwest of Eloth, which was situated at the north end of the Gulf of Aqaba. From there, they passed above the northern end of the gulf and then turned to the southeast along the east shore of the gulf through ancient Midian (modern-day Saudi Arabia), to modern-day Jabel El Lawz, which is ancient Sinai (Horeb). The Habiru, (mixture of the descendants of Abraham by his three wives, Sarah, Hagar, and Keturah) led by Moses, had turned northward through the wadi when God directed Moses to "turn back—and encamp by the sea". (R.S.V. Ex. 14:1) As a result of this change in direction, they found themselves cornered between the impassable mountain, the sea and Pharaoh's army. This event took place on the Gulf of Aqaba and not the Gulf of Suez as most scholars suppose!

We took scuba diving lessons, dove at the site our research led us to, found and photographed several chariot parts! There we were able to observe the underwater "land bridge" which we saw on the map. We later found and retrieved parts of human and animal skeletons, some of which we have had examined by a forensic pathologist for verification. The details, photographs and analysis are included in our forthcoming book, DISCOVERED: ROUTE AND RELICS OF THE 1446 B.C. EXODUS.

During the summer of 1979 I was invited to participate in the opening of a cave at Engedi in Israel. The man who had discovered this cave, by years of dangerous difficult research, Larry Blaser, had arranged for the opening. I arrived en route to eastern Turkey with Rene Noorbergen, whom I had invited to accompany me to the boat formation. The opening was to be done by well-known archaeologist and explorer, Dr. James Strange from F.S.U. and Dr. William Ludgenbill from a university in Michigan. Due to a disagreement over picture rights, and the evaluation of a geologist from Illinois that the cave had never been open to the surface, the attempt was terminated. This decision was approaching when I had to leave for Turkey, so I authorized Rene Noorbergen to offer a reward of $1,000.00 to the first man into the cave. He had decided that the rewards of discovery were potentially greater in Engedi than in eastern Turkey and decided to stay there. After the termination decision, the various participants returned to their homes. I had been convinced by Larry's careful research that the cave contained relics from the past. He hoped to find the Ark of the Covenant and other artifacts from the first temple in the cave, but it was my belief that the cave contained Amorite burials from a period between the third millennium until the time of the conquest of Canaan by the Habiru around 1400 B.C.

While working on the Ark of the Covenant excavation during the winter of 1979-80, we asked for and received permission to do an exploratory look into the cave at Engedi. We designed a device that held a camera at its ten foot end and forced a small opening into the cave. We inserted our camera, took photographs of the interior as best we could and discovered burial crypts cut into the walls of the cave! The facts and photographs of this discovery will appear in our forthcoming book entitled: DISCOVERED: GIANTS.

While attempting to retrieve the remains of chariots and other artifacts from the Red Sea crossing site in the summer of 1978, I acquired a severe sun burn that resulted in the swelling of my feet and legs to a point where it became impossible to wear my diving equipment. We were forced by this circumstance to await our return A.P.E.X. flight home in Jerusalem.

While there, I became acquainted with the manager of a piece of property near the old city. While inspecting the property with him, and to my total shock and dismay, my arm pointed to a site on the property and my mouth said "That is Jeremiah's grotto and the Ark of the Covenant is in there". While I stood in stunned silence, the manager said "That's wonderful! We will let you excavate, provide room and board, do your laundry, and supply all the diggers you need." I mumbled that I couldn't start then but would be glad to in the near future!

Our flight was the next morning, and I was anxious to get home to my books and see if my involuntary pointing and statement were possibly true! My action and statement were accompanied with the nerve tingling sensation that I had come to recognize as an indicator of a supernatural presence. However I had also become aware that a similar nerve tingling sensation can be the results of the presence of evil supernatural beings! My research showed that the Ark had vanished from recorded history during the siege of Jerusalem by Babylon in 587-6 B.C. The city had been surrounded by "forts round about" (a siege wall). It would have been humanly impossible to take the Ark out of the siege wall. This led to the conclusion that the Ark had been hidden in, under, or near the city within the siege wall. When we explained this conclusion to the Israeli officials and showed them our permit from the land owners, they gladly granted us an exploratory permit. Our excitement level ran high as we discovered absolute proof of the location of Christ's crucifixion and burial.

While it will be necessary for you to wait for the details and photographs of most of our discoveries, I will share the most profound discovery of them all. On January 6, 1982 at 2:00 P.M., I entered a chamber that contained the Ark of the Covenant and other furnishings from the first temple!

In Rev. 77:13 we are told that God's way (modus operandi) is in the sanctuary. The sacrificial system given to Adam and Eve, after their fall and eviction from the garden of Eden, was simply the symbolic transfer of mankind's sins from themselves to the lamb, bullock, or turtle dove (based on the wealth of the participant). These creatures represented the sinless Son of God that one day would die in our stead and, in doing so, would make it possible that all could obtain forgiveness of their sins, freedom from human weakness that caused man to sin, and restoration to an immortal existence with our Immortal God. Later, during the Theocracy of Israel, a copy of the heavenly sanctuary was built under the direction of God, and the entire mechanics of the redemptive act of The Deities was acted out. The above described sacrifices were supervised by the priests of the sanctuary, and the guilt of the sinners was symbolically transferred to the HOLY compartment of the sanctuary. One time each year these sins were symbolically transferred from the sanctuary, where they had accumulated for the past year, to the head of a goat. This goat represented Christ as the sinbearer. This goat was killed, and its blood was carried into the MOST HOLY compartment of the sanctuary WHERE IT WAS SPRINKLED "BEFORE" THE ARK OF THE COVENANT. This SYMBOLIZED THE BLOOD OF CHRIST SATISFYING THE CLAIMS OF GOD'S ETERNAL LAW UPON THE LAWBREAKER AND THE SINNER'S ACCEPTANCE BY THE FATHER "IN THE BELOVED" SON.

During the siege of Jerusalem by the Babylonians in 587-6 B.C., God directed Jeremiah and/or some priests to HIDE THE ARK OF THE COVENANT in a cave chamber. Six hundred years later, THE ROMANS CUT CROSS HOLES IN THE STONE DIRECTLY ABOVE THIS CHAMBER and IN ONE OF THESE CROSS HOLES, CHRIST WAS CRUCIFIED. The "STONES WERE RENT" at the moment of His death. A SPLIT IN THE STONE LED FROM THE LEFT SIDE OF THE CROSS HOLE DOWN INTO THE CAVE CHAMBER WHERE THE ARK HAD BEEN SECRETED 600 YEARS BEFORE, AND WHEN THE CENTURION STUCK HIS SPEAR INTO CHRIST'S SIDE, THE BLOOD AND WATER FLOWED DOWN HIS SIDE, DOWN THROUGH THE SPLIT IN THE STONE AND UPON THE MERCY SEAT! IT WAS HERE THAT TYPE MET ANTI-TYPE AND THE SALVATION OF THE HUMAN FAMILY WAS ASSURED! You will be able to see all this on video and in photographs in the near future "IN GOD'S TIME".

CHAPTER 7

OBSERVATIONS AND REMARKS BY CRITICS AND SUPPORTERS (ON NOAH'S ARK)

This section will deal with direct quotations of both critics and supporters of the work I've done:

1) From THE ARK, A REALITY? by Richard C. Bright, p. 25.

"CONCLUSION: It is my opinion the boat shaped object near Tendurek is not Noah's Ark . . . "

COMMENTS: Richard's book is an excellent account of the Ark searches, past and present. While he doesn't agree that this is the Ark, he presents an informative and detailed account of his participation with Jim Irwin in his expeditions.

2) From THE ARARAT REPORT, Bill Crouse, Editor, May-June 1988, "Ron Wyatt: Are His Claims Bona Fide?" pp 7 & 9.

"So, should Christians celebrate what could be the most monumental archaeological discovery since the Dead Sea Scrolls?

Again, from our perspective, we think it would be very premature to do so. As we have briefly pointed out, we have yet to see ANY evidence that would be definitive.

To us, it seems incredible that Ron could have found and solved problems that have baffled professional archaeologists for more than a century. We think Ron missed his calling. He could be a "can't lose" writer for episodes of "Indiana Jones" movies.

As a Christian I can't think of anything that would be more exciting than to learn of the discovery of Noah's Ark. And, if Ron turns out to be right, you'd better believe we'll be among the first to apologize for doubting his claims."

3) From THE ARK OF NOAH, by David Fasold, p. 23 and 24.

"I broke open the frequency generator and Samran came alongside me, robes flowing white on white against the snow . . . I'd forgotten my glasses as well as my lunch, and the numbers focused slowly as I dialed in the number for iron."

'Ron, you are crossing longitudinal walls, or floor beams that contain decomposed iron fittings, maybe nails, or brackets of some kind.' My voice was raising higher in excitement. 'They are so evenly spaced I could measure the distance between them. What do you think they are, Ron?' I said, moving in for a close-up to catch the emotion of the moment.

Ron just stood there, grinning from ear to ear. 'I don't know, maybe rows of cages . . .' he started to say.

'Come on, Ron, do you think you're on Noah's Ark?'

'Hey, fella,' he broke into a sigh of relief, 'I always said this was Noah's Ark!'

I turned to find the mayor of the village with the question still on his face. 'Evet (yes), Nuh'un Gemisi,' I shouted in joy, and his eyes broke into a smile of tears."

COMMENT: David called me in 1985 after Jim Irwin had referred him to me. He's called Jim and told him of his belief that the Ark couldn't be on Mt. Ararat and asked Jim about the possibility of his doing radar scans at the foot of the mountain. I must credit David with introducing the electronic equipment which allowed us to "see" the inside structural remains. David also accompanied me to Saudi Arabia right after the trip referred to in the above quote, when I was invited to return at royal request, and show the Saudi archaeologists the site of the real Mt. Sinai.

4) From THE INSTITUTE OF JUDAIC-CHRISTIAN RESEARCH, INC. RESEARCH LETTER, Vendyl Jones Ministries, November 1987, p. 1, and September 1988, p. 1

"The search is over—Successfully over! Noah's Ark has been found over 6,000 feet above sea level, seventeen miles southeast of Mt. Ararat. In 1985, Ark-eologist, David Fasold, filed his report *with the government of Turkey. The Turkish government closed the area off with the army while their own archaeologists made an investigation of David Fasold's report."*

I will refrain from giving the almost unbelievable details of David Fasold's find. I think he should do that since he is the one who found Noah's Ark.

David's find is in complete agreement with the Bible and other historic sources. Dr. M. Salih Bayraktutan, Turkish geologist, says the boat shaped object is not natural in situ but is an anomaly to the surrounding geological environment. My impression and opinion is that it is the fossil of Noah's Ark. Salih also stated: 'Mt. Big Ararat was volcanic and if the Ark landed there it would be under four to five thousand feet of lava. Furthermore, the hydrodynamics of a cone shape volcanic mountain would push the Ark away from it.' "

COMMENT: Mr. Jones gives David Fasold credit for the discovery.

5) From "THE DISCOVERY CHANNEL MAGAZINE", "Raiders's of Noah's Ark" by Kit Carlson, October 1988, p. 10.

"A team of West German and Turkish mountain climbers tackle these questions along with Ararat's slippery slopes in THE SECRET OF MT. ARARAT, premiering this month on the Discovery Channel. Although the team's primary focus is to reach the peak of this treacherous mountain, along the way they explore some of the claims that have been made by other ark-seekers.

The most compelling claim they find is one made by Ron Wyatt, a 55-year-old Nashville anesthetist. Since 1977, Wyatt has been examining a huge, boat shaped earth formation located on a plateau 15 kilometers below the mountain's peak. He is convinced he has found Noah's Ark."

6) Quotation by DR. NATHAN MEYER, President of the Bible Prophecy Association who travelled with me to see Noah's Ark in June of 1988.

"I've been involved in the search for Noah's Ark ever since 1970 (with the Search Foundation). At that time I thought, as did a lot of others, that the Ark was high on the icy slopes of Big Ararat.

But after visiting this site with Ron in the summer of '88, I was compelled to change my mind. Even though we don't have the absolute proof as yet, the evidences he presented are rather overwhelming and difficult to refute.

I must say it looks like this is the real thing."

7) From THE NASHVILLE BANNER, "Turkish Team Believes Find is Noah's Ark" by Clarke Canfield, Dec. 1986.

"A Turkish research team has concurred with a Madison explorer's claim that the remains of Noah's Ark are buried on a barren mountainside in eastern Turkey.

Two government officials, one at the Turkish consulate in New York and another in Ankara, the Turkish capital, said top government officials will meet this month to discuss what steps to take to document and preserve what the research team says is a priceless discovery."

"The Department of Ministry and Tourism has been ready to make the area a national park and declare it is Noah's Ark, based on the evidence presented by various researchers,' Turkish Tourism Consul Kamil Muren said from New York.

'No official confirmation has been forwarded to me yet,' he said. 'But in the Holy Book and the Koran, it is mentioned that Noah's Ark is located in that area.'

'Nobody has any doubts about it (being Noah's Ark)'."

"Government officials in Turkey are hesitant to talk publicly about the research team's report, but will meet December 12th in Ankara to decide what to do with it, according to Mine Uneler, a Turkish Government liaison and interpreter.

Ms. Uneler, who works for the Ministry of the Interior and served as an interpreter and liaison between Wyatt and the Ministry of Culture and Tourism in Ankara, said the government has concluded the object is indeed Noah's Ark.

'Our government exactly agrees with Mr. Wyatt, said Ms. Uneler, adding the December 12th conference will include officials from

the departments of foreign affairs and internal affairs and researchers from Ataturk University."

"Wyatt has made numerous journeys to Turkey with scientists, explorers, and others, including Irwin, over the years studying the various sites in search of the elusive Ark.

He said in 1977 he found the Ark but nobody believed him. But by the summer of 1985, he had apparently convinced others of the validity of that site.

It was then that the Turkish government closed off the area to the public to conduct its own studies of the area.

John Baumgardner, a geophysicist from the National Laboratory in Los Alamos, New Mexico, has made several trips to Turkey in recent years and is convinced the Ark is where Wyatt says it is.

Baumgardner said that when the Turkish government closed off the area in 1985, he asked an official with the Office of Foreign Affairs why they were restricting the area.

'He said it was because of the potential of this being a very important archaeological site,' Baumgardner said.

He said he had also been informed about the research team's report.

'The report says these researchers believe these are the remains of Noah's Ark and recommend that the area be turned into a national park,' Baumgardner said.

In October, a Turkish newspaper published what the researchers' report said about the Ark and printed the headline "Nuh'un Gemisi burada" (Noah's Ark is here) with a picture of the site below it."

8) Written quotation by GREG BREWER, noted prophecy writer and lecturer, July 11, 1989

"I am like so many others who, upon hearing this incredible news, was a bit skeptical. I have examined all the evidence, and I am fully convinced this is the Ark of Noah. It is my opinion that each man has a gift which God has given to him to use for the glory of God; in Ron's case it is in archaeology.

I am not a scientist so I will not comment on the technical aspects of the find. I can comment on the man, Ron Wyatt. I see true Christianity at work here with an obsession for honesty in all his affairs and to be led by prayer and the Spirit. I know my Bible pretty well, and there is no subject of which Ron is not familiar with. This shows me there have been many deep hours of study and prayer to get this kind of Bible knowledge. It is his desire to see many souls won to Christ as a result of proving by archaeology the Bible account of the past is a true one. It is my unchangeable belief that Ron's work is a gift of God's mercy to this last doubting generation who seeks a sign."

CHAPTER 8

QUOTES AND COMMENTS ON THE DISCOVERY OF THE RED SEA CROSSING SITE AND THE REAL MT. SINAI

Shortly after my first trip to Turkey in 1977, when it became apparent that I couldn't do much regarding the Ark, I was impressed to begin work on the Red Sea crossing site. After the discoveries there, I knew positively that Mt. Sinai was in Saudi Arabia. Being unable to get a visa after almost four years, the only way to get there was to chance entry without one. And while it cost my sons and I almost three months in prison, we found Mt. Sinai. I took my information to others I knew had the connections and ability to obtain legal entry. While we originally agreed to visit the site together, they ended up making the trip alone. However, it appears that with the map and details I furnished them, they were able to photograph the site and bring the photos back with them.

Now, in order that the glory and credit go to the Lord, I feel it my duty to make it known that it was God who led me there. Not my wisdom or the wisdom of others. If different men made each discovery, Noah's Ark, the Red Sea crossing site with the chariot parts, the real Mt. Sinai, and the Ark of the Covenant, people could say they were just lucky or really did their research. But one person could not find all these things without divine leading. It is for this reason that I present the following quotes.

1) From TREASURES OF THE LOST RACES, by Rene Noorbergen, copyrighted in 1982, pp. 163 - 166.

"The theory on which Ron Wyatt was basing his exploratory trip into the Middle East was founded on two very obvious points made by Flavius Josephus and recorded in the Bible. Both mention that the Hebrew children went south from Egypt, through the desert,

ending at the shore of the Red Sea in an area where 'the mountains were closed with the sea.' That the Red Sea at that time extended, in name at least, as far as Eilat at the top of the Gulf of Aqaba can be seen in I Kings 9:26, where it states that 'King Solomon made a navy of ships in Ezion-geber, which is beside Eloth, on the shore of the Red Sea, in the land of Edom.'

Wyatt reasoned therefore that the Israelites had crossed the Sinai from west to east and had finally reached an area on the eastern coast (Gulf of Aqaba) where a mountain range met the sea. According to the record, the Egyptians had taken over the mountain peaks near the area to prevent the Hebrews from escaping. It also mentions that after they had crossed the Red Sea, Moses took them to 'Mt. Sinai in order to offer sacrifices to God.'

A careful examination of the eastern shore of the Sinai peninsula allows for only one place where two million people and their flocks can be gathered. It is the wide expanse of beach near Nuweba, the south end of which is closed off by steep mountains! Nearby is a wide and wild mountain gorge known as the Wadi Watir, an ancient dried-out riverbed that forms a natural roadway into the Sinai desert. What's more, the traditional Mt. Sinai is deep within the Sinai desert, while both the Bible and Josephus indicate that Moses took the Hebrews to Mt. Sinai after they crossed the Red Sea into what is now known as Arabia. Interestingly, not far from the opposite shore is a mountain known as Jabel El Lawz, a steep, forbidding peak. Is it perhaps possible that this is the Mt. Sinai that Moses speaks of? There are many different theories regarding the possible location of the real Mt. Sinai, and Ron Wyatt's location wasn't all that farfetched. He held that the Israelites, after leaving Egypt, went down the western side of the Sinai along the Gulf of Suez and crossed the Sinai from west to east through its most rugged mountainous section by travelling over the dried-out riverbeds that run into each other. Their route, according to him, could well have gone via the Wadi Feiran, connecting with the Wadi El Akhdar, which in turn runs into the Wadi Salaqa, becomes the Wadi Zaranek, and eventually meets the Gulf of Aqaba via the well- known Wadi Watir. The Wadi Watir is the only wadi that ends at a wide beach-like expanse whose southernmost end is cut off by steep mountains.

44

An escaping horde of people arriving at the Red Sea via the Wadi Watir had only two choices: to be annihilated on the beach by the pursuing armies that could enclose it from the north, while it was hemmed in by mountains on the west and south; or to go forward into the water. There simply could have been no other."

2) From THE CBS MORNING NEWS with Bill Kurtis and Diane Sawyer, Tuesday April 17, 1984.

BILL KURTIS: "Three weary Americans came home Monday night; Ronald Wyatt and his sons, Daniel and Ronald, Jr., at the end of an amateur archaeology expedition that landed them in a Saudi Arabian jail. They entered Saudi Arabia illegally, searching for the site of the Biblical Mt. Sinai. Repeated requests for a legal visa were turned down, so the Wyatts slipped across the Jordanian border, only to be arrested by Saudi police as they were heading back. Now what followed was a hair-raising 75 days in custody.

Ronald Wyatt and his sons are with us in the studios of our Nashville affiliate, WTVF, to tell you all about it.

Gentlemen, good morning!

RONALD WYATT AND SONS: Good morning!

BILL KURTIS: Uh, Mr. Wyatt, you there in the middle, your sons on either side, why did you, . . . uh, I didn't know that Mt. Sinai was in Saudi Arabian territory! Why did you think it was?

RONALD WYATT: We found some chariot parts that looked like the chariots found in King Tut's tomb in the Gulf of Aqaba, west of this Jabel El Lawz. Now, we found these at depths from 60 feet out to 200 feet and over a stretch of about a mile and a half. And we believe that was the crossing site, so in the Biblical narrative, they arrived at Mt. Sinai after crossing the Red Sea. The language in the Bible indicated that they stayed 'in' a mountain; enclosed in a mountain. So, an aerial map showed that this Jabel El Lawz had a large valley enclosed in the rim of an ancient volcano. There's about 5,000 acres in there. We felt this was the place. And, in Exodus 24:4 and Leviticus 6:28, 11:33 and 15:12, it tells of some artifacts that were to be found. There would be twelve pillars of stone and an altar and some pottery, and so this is why we looked

45

at that particular mountain.

3) Direct quote from DAVID FASOLD regarding his accompaniment with Ron on the April, 1985 visit to Saudi Arabia, July 16, 1989.

"On April 2, 3 and 4 of 1985, an archaeological survey was conducted by Mr. Ronald Wyatt of Madison, Tennessee, at Jabel El Lawz, Kingdom of Saudi Arabia. The molecular survey, leading to points of interest, was carried out by Mr. David Fasold of Port Salerno, Florida, who accompanied Mr. Wyatt and Samran Al-Moteiri, a prominent citizen of Tabuk, who had gained permission to conduct the survey. The purpose of the investigation was that Mr. Wyatt's premise that the mountain, Jabel El Lawz, represented the true Mt. Sinai in the land of Midian, which is, of course, in northern Arabia, and not in the Sinai Peninsula.

The site is located some 144 kilometers by road from Tabuk towards Hagl. When soon after crossing a bridge, a dry wadi is followed west for a distance of 48.7 kilometers.

Upon questioning a bedouin in the area if this was indeed Jabel El Lawz, Ibrahim Salem Frich responded with "nahm, Jabel Musa henna!", which means "yes, the mountain of Moses is here!"

The bedouin showed us the remains of a temple that, during the reign of Sulyimin, the Turkish "Sulyimin, the great", had been stripped of cut stone for building material for a mosque in Hagl. I would have liked to have seen this mosque to ascertain how many blocks were removed from the site, but time did not permit.

25 rectangular blocks, 16½" by 8¼", varying in length from 26¼" to 39", were scattered at the site below a raised platform, and 10 pillar sections are visible, varying in height from 10" to 26" with a 22¾" diameter. The temple platform represents ¼ of a circle leading from a set of three pools joined to a large rock best described as the size of an "up-ended" car, which carries slightly incised, esoteric symbols. This site nestles between two mountains.

Closer to the wadi, the molecular survey uncovered a line of 12 circles of stone with an outside diameter of 18 feet, consisting of three rows of stones in thickness. It would appear to this writer that the construction was not a "shaft grave" or walls for wells, but the remains of standing towers. The 12 were spaced five feet apart from one another in a straight line bearing 193 degrees magnetic. The elevation at this site is 4,050 feet, some 20 feet above the wadi, 70 feet below the temple remains and less than ⅛ of a mile distance from the temple; from tower number four, Jabel El Lawz bearing 216 degrees and the other mountain at 270 degrees.

Directly across the wadi, a survey line was followed to a low grouping of stones that were covered with petroglyphs in the following manner: an area of the stone was washed with a substance that was absorbed by the rock about 1/8 of an inch; a pointed tool was then employed that, when struck against the blackened rock to a depth of 1/4 of an inch, left a white mark. The artist thus portrayed images of Hathor and Apis, the Egyptian sacred cows, in dotted outline with their markings, in several cases, six figures apiece.

When shown to an archaeologist sent from Riyad University to verify the site, Wyatt was congratulated on the discovery and the area promptly closed. All photographs were confiscated.

Two visits to the site in the spring of 1988 by Larry Williams, an explorer from Rancho Santa Fe, California, verified by photograph that the petroglyph site was now enclosed by a 12 foot, chain link fence and barbed wire, with a large blue and white 4 foot by 8 foot sign in the Arabic and English that it was a protected site of historical importance. Two other sites, the temple and the towers, are protected by the same type fence, encircling two entire mountains.

This writer feels that the cost involved in the fencing alone shows that the Saudis are taking this site very seriously.

This writer feels there are numerous problems with identifying the site as the "Mountain of Moses", as well as the traditional site on the peninsula. But until further examination, it remains a mystery.

Certainly, the 12 towers in connection with what is undoubtedly petroglyphs of Egyptian origin in the land of Midian should raise interest. I can assure you that this was Wyatt's first trip to the site, but not his first attempt. I can personally verify that the discoveries were made in accordance with the theory formulated by

Wyatt that the Exodus route from the Egyptians crossed the eastern arm of the Red Sea, into Midian and returning to Mt. Horeb - Jabel El Lawz.

Signed,

David Fasold"

4) From THE WALL STREET JOURNAL, "Larry Williams Hit Contest Home Run But His Clients Could Still Strike Out" by John R. Dorfman, May 1989.

"Consider the case of Larry R. Williams, a swing-for-the-fences commodity trader. In a 1987 contest, he parlayed a $10,000 stake into more that $1 million."

"He had twice won the Republican nomination for a U.S. Senate seat from Montana, though he lost the general elections and later moved to California. He recently made an expedition to Saudi Arabia, where, he claims, he and his colleagues found the true site of the Biblical Mount Sinai."

COMMENT: I called Larry when I heard they had made the trip, and he informed me that the photos had been turned over to Harvard University for study. That is all he told me.

5) From HIGH FLIGHT FOUNDATION NEWSLETTER, Headed by Jim Irwin "Report by Bob Cornuke on Noah's Ark and Mt. Sinai", July 1988

"Great news! We strongly feel that the real Mt. Sinai has been discovered. Since February, we have been searching in Egypt and Saudi Arabia in an attempt to find the real Mt. Sinai, currently believed to be in Egypt. The Bible, however, is quite clear that Mt. Sinai is in Arabia (Galatians 4:25). We have found an underwater land bridge in the Red Sea in the area of the tip of the Sinai Peninsula. This land bridge was photographed and found to be a perfect underwater bridge to Arabia.

Larry Williams and I have taken two trips to Saudi Arabia and traveled to Jabel Al Lawz. This mountain is believed by some Biblical

48

scholars to possibly be the real Mt. Sinai. Jabel Al Lawz is an 8,000 ft. mountain with a huge valley at its base. In this valley we found an ancient altar with petroglyphs of the Egyptian bull god, Hathor, inscribed in the rocks. We feel this is the altar where Aaron made the Golden Calf. There were also very strong readings of the mineral gold registered at this site."

CHAPTER 9

THE LIVING WORD

After I arrived at the conclusion that the Bible was exactly what It claimed to be, the Word of the Living God, I put the God of that Word to the test. This is what He invites you and I to do. A careful reading of the book of Acts quickly convinced me of the undeniable fact that the early believers had a working relationship with their God and were used of Him in a startling manner to win lost souls to Him. The tragic truth is that I have lived among professed Christians most of my life and have seen none of the evidences of the love and power of God demonstrated in and through them. What I have seen on television, in the pulpit and in the dealings of professed Christians, is towering human pride, selfishness, a publicly professed hatred of sinners and a private love and participation in the very sins they so vehemently denounce publicly. Rare indeed is an encounter with anyone whose actions reveal anything more than a pretended religion. Converts are sought for no other purpose than to bring praise to the evangelist and add money to the coffers of the churches.

Little or none of these monies are used to feed the hungry, clothe the naked, provide shelter for the homeless and care for the sick and dying. Instead these monies are used to build magnificent buildings and to support a lifestyle among the "merchandisers of the Grace of God" that is totally different from that of our "example who had not where to lay His head." Reader, these people are not God's representatives in a sin-sick world that is teetering on the very brink of destruction! You must look to where there are those who in humility and fear (respect) of God and a deep abiding love for those for whom Christ died; I speak not of the "multi-national organizations" who ask for money over the television and skim 98% of the donations to feed, clothe and care for the sick and needy, for "administrative costs."

In the day of judgment God will say, *"Verily I say unto you, Inasmuch as ye have done it unto one of the least of these My brethren, ye have done it unto Me."* Matthew 25:40. To the pretenders through whom Satan performed his "signs and lying wonders" God says, *"Verily I say unto you, Inasmuch as ye did it not to one of the least of these, ye did it not to me."* Matthew 25:45. *"I never knew you: depart from Me, ye that work iniquity."* Matthew 7:23. God further says, *"Pure religion and undefiled before God and the Father is this, To visit the fatherless and widows in their affliction, and to keep himself unspotted from the world."* James 1:27. Friend, if this is not your lifestyle, your eternal life and those for whom you should be laboring are in deadly peril.

If these are strong words to your ears, if you feel discomfort as you read them, this is a good sign. We are created by a magnificent God who gave us the ability not only to choose, but the ability to know the truth when we hear it. The world has lost sight of many of the great truths, but to those who thirst for them, He will not disappoint you.

And many times we may not recognize the truth for it is not what we were looking for. We have preconceived notions as to what we need to know and want to hear. Consider the disciples; they were able to go forth into a world set on their destruction and preach the gospel with profound effect and determination. They had unfaltering faith because of their living, breathing experience with the Lord. They came and followed Him; they listened as he preached; they recognized the truth, and they believed. Then, when all appeared lost, when their precious master hung on a cross as a common criminal instead of reigning from His earthly throne over His earthly kingdom, they felt their very hearts torn from them. Yet, when it seemed as though darkness would prevail, Christ arose from the dead and came to them, a living testimony to our promise of salvation and victory over death. God alone, in His wisdom, knew exactly how to bring about the kind of conviction within the disciples needed to carry the gospel to the world.

I also have experienced God and cannot tread lightly in presenting the message that must be heard. In my studies I've noted more and more that scholars are promoting the belief that there wasn't a true exodus. One writer stated that he believed it had to be a slow migration over a period of many years for there wasn't any evidence of millions of people journeying through the stated path. Egyptologists flatly state that there is no evidence of Moses in Egyptian history, and therefore he was just a Hebrew folk-hero. Imagine their faces when they discover the positive evidences of not only who Moses was in Egyptian history but who his adoptive mother was, who the pharaoh was that died in the Red Sea and who was the first-born son of pharaoh that died in the plagues! Note Jeremiah 16:14 - *"Therefore, behold the days come, saith the Lord, that it shall no more be said, The Lord liveth that brought up the children of Israel out of the land of Egypt."* As far as I can ascertain, our present age is the first time this disbelief has existed. Even the Moslems devoutly believe in Moses.

But there is no doubt that it all happened exactly as the Lord preserved it in the Holy Scriptures. I can assure you, for in 1978 I saw with my own eyes the chariot wheels on the sea floor, some gold-plated, some iron, some still attached to the axles, and in 1984 I saw Mt. Sinai in Saudi Arabia, with the altar, 12 pillars and everything written of in Exodus 24:4 and more. My sons and I spent 75 days in prison there after we were reported to the Saudi Arabian Embassy as being Israeli spies by someone I had trusted and confided in. Our release and return home was televised on the CBS Morning News, and we told the country of our discovery. No one said they didn't believe us, but if they had, would they have just smiled and gone on to the next news story? It would have been very easy to be discouraged at that point in my life. Prison is never pleasant, especially when your two sons are with you and you realize that you may be there a very long time. But when we were released and our captors told us the name of the person who had reported us to be spies, it was a disillusionment in my fellow man that brought perhaps my deepest personal awareness of how vile Satan really is. It also was another living experience of the power of God. When things looked their bleakest and we had almost given up hope, we were set free. And it was also perhaps my greatest test, for as Christ had loved and died for every sinner, even those who condemned and crucified him, I was commanded to love even this man. Only through God's love and might are we able to love those who persecute us.

"Therefore, behold, I will this once cause them to know Mine Hand and My might and they shall know that My name is the Lord." Jeremiah 16:19.

God is about to open everyone's eyes. *'The Lord is not slack concerning His promise, as some men count slackness; but is longsuffering to us-ward, not willing that any should perish, but that all should come to repentance."* 2 Peter 3:9. When it is His time, and not a minute sooner, things will be revealed to you that will cause you to know that the events of the Bible happened exactly as God spoke it through His divinely inspired writers.

We need only to look around us to know that Satan is intensely aroused against the Word of God. He knows the scriptures well and therefore knows what lies ahead for him and his fallen angels. He is going to wage great warfare on any light we receive and we must each be aware. Many may preach things that "sound right" or "make a lot of sense", but check it out for yourself in the Word of God! *'There is a way that seemeth right unto a man, but the end thereof are the ways of death."* Proverbs 16:25. Cling to His promise - *"If any of you lack wisdom, let him ask of God that giveth to all men liberally, and upbraideth not and it shall be given him."* James 1:5.

CHAPTER 10

MY TESTIMONY

The following experiences are highlights of my personal relationship with our wonderful and caring Lord. Before God, who cannot lie and to whom lying lips are an abomination, I present these experiences to you as real and the substance of my deep love and humble gratitude to Him, who with His son *"freely gives us all things."* Romans 8:32, and who *"is able to do exceeding abundantly above all that we ask or think, . . ."* Ephesians 3:20.

As I became aware of the reality of God, I prayed that if it was not asking too much, He would allow me to have a dream in which I could see the earth restored or perhaps even heaven. Several years later, after I had prayed for this three or four times and had become convinced it wasn't His will, I had a vivid, "technicolor" dream; I was floating noiselessly through the air above a body of crystal clear water. The water appeared to be "alive" with multicolored and variously shaped fish and other creatures. Then, I looked up and all around and saw mounds of grass and flower-covered earth protruding from the water. On each of the mounds grew a massive tree whose amazingly long, low branches spread out in all directions and touched the tips of identical branches extending from similar trees on the numerous other mounds. The leaves and branches seemed alive with breathtakingly colored birds and butterflies. After awhile, I became aware of the silence, the absence of any "motor" noise, and suddenly wondered what was propelling me up and over the water. Looking up, down and all around, I saw that I was simply floating through the air. I then looked ahead and saw that the water ended in a profusion of breathtaking flowering vegetation that included lilies, cattails and many others unfamiliar to me. Beyond these, a luxurious, multicolored valley with predominantly green and yellow vegetation swept away from me and upward to dark green hued mountains. I awoke immediately thanked our Heavenly Father for His kindness in answering a sinner's prayer.

Some time after this first dream and well into the hectic events involving Noah's ark, the Red Sea crossing, how Joseph built the Step Pyramid for the pharaoh of the seven year famine, the site of the real Mt. Sinai, and several seasons of excavation that led to the discovery of the Ark of the Covenant and several other startling evidences of the crucifixion site, I was struck with a deep depression. Being aware of how God had miraculously helped me locate the remains of evidences and artifacts from every major event of the Bible, I was struck with the impossibility of my being able to handle the complicated business of getting the facts out to the people along with the significance of each discovery in the end times of earth's history. In a state of abject discouragement, I fell asleep and again, dreamed.

In this dream, I was in some unknown location high upon a ledge or something where it was possible to look out and see the entire world with its cities, seas and people. The people were scurrying about like millions of ants on an anthill. For some reason, I looked about for a means to get to the highest point from which I might shout and hopefully get some of their atten- tion. To my left and high up on the side of a nearly sheer cliff face was a narrow ledge. Without hesitation, I decided to attempt to climb it. The loose stones and rocks under my feet began to slip and slide as I climbed. After what seemed like an eternity, I finally reached the ledge, pulled myself up carefully and turned around. I shouted "JESUS IS COMING!" The loudness and intonation sounded exactly right to me. Suddenly, everyone stopped scurrying about and stood looking right at me! Then, gradually the frenzied activity began again, and the greater part of the people passed from my view. All that was left were a few small groups and individuals who continued to stand and watch. The dream ended, and upon awaking I realized that God adds whatever is necessary to our own feeble efforts to accomplish His purpose. I also was deeply impressed with the reality that while God's last message would be heard and understood by all, only a relative few would "love" the truth; *"And with all deceivableness of unrighteousness in them that perish; because they received not the love of the truth, that they might be saved."* II Thessalonians 2:10. The majority would "love and believe lies" and therefore be lost.

"And as it was in the days of Noe, so shall it be also in the days of the Son of man." Luke 17:26.

As was my custom, in the early hours of December 22, 1980, I asked God for the privilege of witnessing to someone whom He knew to be ready to be witnessed to. I prayed that He would have me to say exactly what they needed to hear. I further prayed for the privilege of helping someone that was in real need. I have discovered that I am mostly unable to distinguish between those who are truly needy and those who are "professional beggars." After this prayer, I was strongly impressed to drive to Columbia, Kentucky, a town that was a good two and one half hours drive in good weather. However, the night before, a blizzard had hit Nashville, Tennessee, where I lived, and every road in and out of town was closed. I was on duty at Donelson Hospital for "in- house" O.B. anesthesia administration and wasn't too sure if my relief would be able to make it in. I silently prayed that when I called the state police office to check on the roads, if they said all the roads were closed, I wouldn't go. I called. Their reply was "unless it is a life or death situation, stay off the roads." I knew without hesitation that I was to go. Not knowing what I was to do or who it would be for, I brought along three copies of a book I found to be a marvelous presentation of the plan of salvation, and my small, marked Bible and set out.

I only saw four cars along the approximately 120 miles. Two of these were stopped in the middle of the road; one was a motorist with a wheel broken from his car, and the other was a highway patrolman helping this motorist. My

1976 Dodge Maxi Van had chronic fan belt problems with a great deal of overheating problems. After several long hours of miserable driving, I arrived in Columbia. The slippery road conditions convinced me of my need for a set of studded snow tires on the back of the van, so I pulled into the Columbia Tire Shop, bought a set and had them mounted. Still not having any idea who I was to witness to, I struck up a conversation with the owner of the shop. We discussed world events and some religious subjects, but the encounter didn't seem to warrant such a difficult trip through ice and snow. So, just in case this was why I had been sent here, I give him one of the copies of the books, "The Story of Redemption", I had brought. He thanked me for the book, I paid for the tires and left. What now? Where was I to go? I decided that a cup of hot coffee would feel mighty good right then, so I pulled into a restaurant. I chatted with the waitress. Again the topics were world events and a little on religious subjects, but I doubted this was the encounter God had lined up; I gave her a copy of the book just in case. It began to get dark, and the return trip to Nashville began to weigh heavily on my mind. I believed the purpose of my trip hadn't been accomplished, but with the long, cold trip ahead and the absence of a single clue as to my mission, I decided to finish my coffee and be on my way.

I paid my tab and got in my van. The parking lot tilted toward the street, and I figured it would be easy to get out of the snow there. It started o.k., but as I attempted to back out, the tires spun and slipped to the side. It wouldn't budge. I got out to see what the problem was. After living in Michigan for many years, I usually had no problem getting myself or others around in the snow and getting "stuck" vehicles out of ditches. As I carefully examined the van, I knew there was <u>no earthly reason for the van to be stuck.</u> After spending about 30 minutes trying to get out, I gave up and went in for some soup and coffee to warm me up. Embarrassed, I sat down and ordered. People came over and offered to help me, but in my humiliation I said "thanks" and just sat a while and ate. Secretly, deep down inside, down where we all live, I began to resent the whole day's business, especially the humiliation of not being able to get in the van and drive out like the few others who came and went while I sat. For forty-five minutes I sat there, my resentment secretly smoldering, when I received a very strong impression to get in the van and go home. I felt a twinge of guilt over my attitude, but not knowing what else to do, I went to the van, started the engine and backed out into the street as if nothing had ever happened! I headed in the direction of the interstate that would take me home.

As I drove carefully along the west-bound lane of the toll road, my conscience began to trouble me more. There wasn't anything I could do except go back and try again, however it would have been illegal to drive back to the exit on the wrong side of the highway, and the next exit was 22 miles west. I began to pray that God would forgive me for my willfulness and please not let someone go without what He had wanted me to do just because I was a jerk. Suddenly, from the median of the toll road staggered a dark form, falling and struggling to get to the side I was travelling on. Slowing down to see if it was a hurt animal, I realized it was a person! With a feeble wave of one arm, he signalled me to stop.

Unable to stop quickly on the snow and ice, I had to slowly back up to where he was. I swung open the passenger door and told him to get in. He was badly frozen; his hands and arms were blue up to where they disappeared into the sleeves of his lightweight coat. The point of his chin, his eyebrows, the tips of his ears and nose were white, indicating near frostbite. As I helped him climb into the van, I asked him what he was doing out there without a car. His speech slurred; I at first thought him to be drunk, but I remembered that extreme cold thickens the tongue and slurs the speech. He slowly raised his arm and pointed to the median; he <u>had</u> a car was what he was trying to say. Jumping out of the van, I crossed to where he had pointed and sure enough, buried deep in the snow, sat a red compact car. I returned to the van and told him I'd take him to the next exit and he could get a wrecker to tow it out. I could tell this distressed him.

"Please, mister, help me get it out; it's three days until Christmas, and twenty-three dollars is every penny I have in this world! I need it for my wife and children's Christmas."

"There's no way we can get it out of there," I told him. "And I don't have a chain or shovel."

"Would you please just try?" he pleaded.

He had a chain in the trunk of his car and thought maybe I could pull him out with it. Totally forgotten was the reason for my trip and the guilt at my apparent failure. Still uncomfortably cold from the day's activities, I waded through the snow to where his car was all but buried. Clearing the snow from the top and sides, I opened the trunk and retrieved the chain. Digging the snow from beneath the back of the car, I securely fastened the chain around the back axle and stretched the free end to the edge of the road. It just barely reached to where I could secure it to the trailer hitch on the van after maneuvering it to that edge of the road. This accomplished, I silently prayed, "Father, if you want this car out of the snow, You are going to have to do it. I sure can't."

At that exact moment, down the east lane of the road, which had been entirely free of traffic during my trip, appeared the headlights of two cars.

"Where did they come from?", the man echoed my surprise. Maybe we had been too busy to notice, but we both thought it strange, for the headlights of two cars are not easy to miss in the dark of a snow-covered landscape such as this.

The two cars slowed to a stop; there was no need for them to pull over to the side as there was no traffic. Four husky young men got out of each car.

"Can we help you?" one of them asked in a friendly

tone.

"Yes; please!" we both resounded.

There were no women, no children or older men in either car; just the eight young men. Strange, I thought, but we couldn't ask for better help. The men waded to the car, placed their hands upon it and signalled for me to pull with the van. Within seconds, the car was up on the road.

"A piece of cake" someone said.

"Thank you, thank you.." we both said.

"You are welcome," we heard as the young men headed back to their cars, brushed the snow from their clothing and got in. They drove off to the east and, puzzled about missing their approach, I watched them leave. As they approached a dip in the highway, the cars slowly disappeared from sight. However, they never arose from that dip! There was no exit for at least two miles, and they hadn't turned around; they had simply vanished into thin air! I remembered Psalms 34:7 as I silently thanked our Father, "The angel of the Lord encampeth round about them that fear Him, and delivereth them."

I cleared the snow from his engine, especially from around the spark plugs and ignition wires. I got in, and it started easily. After a short test drive, I left the motor running, got out and climbed into the van where the man was sitting. I told him it was ready and I would follow him to the next exit.

"My hands won't work. Do you mind if I warm up a little while longer?"

"Of course" I replied. To save his gas, I got out and turned off his car, returned to the van and commented on what good fortune we had had.

"Do you believe in God, mister?" he asked me with almost pleading eyes.

Over an hour later, we had reviewed all the Bible texts on all his questions. I read to him with my fingers moving along the text so he could read along also. Finally, he briskly wiggled his fingers and said he was ready to go.

60

"Would you mind if I say a little prayer for you before you go?" I asked.

"Please, . . . please do." he said.

I prayed for him and his family and thanked God for helping us get his car out. When I opened my eyes, he was crying. With tears rolling down his face, he told me this was the best Christmas of his entire life. He explained how he drove the toll road every weekend to and from his work and how today as he returned home he had been driving along wondering if there was anything to God, religion and the Bible. Then, without warning, his car had just swerved into the snowbank down inside the median. After two hours of waiting, no one had come along, and he had finally decided he was going to die right there in the snow. He told me how he prayed that if God was real, that He please take care of his family. Now, he knew for certain; God was real!

He asked me how he could explain all of this to his family, and I gave him my last copy of "The Story of Redemption." Suddenly, I realized what this trip had been all about.

Another time when I prayed the witnessing prayer was as I was returning from a weekend of continuing education classes in Williamsburg, Virginia. Driving along Interstate 81/VA and enjoying the beautiful scenery, I suddenly noticed my fuel gauge sitting on empty. I decided to pull into the right hand lane and get off at the next exit to "gas up". I passed a sign that said "Next Exit - 3 Miles". After I moved into the right lane, I found there were three cars ahead of me, all travelling about 45 miles per hour, so I decided I had plenty of time to pass them and still get back into the right hand lane to exit. When I pulled out to pass, the middle of the three cars pulled out in front of me and sped up even with the first car and held that position. Then, the third car pulled up even with me. I wouldn't have believed it was possible for a driver, who wanted to exit an interstate with two miles to maneuver before the exit, to get boxed in where it was impossible for him to make his exit without risking an accident. But I know first hand, no; it is.

As we crept past the exit, I breathed a prayer that the Lord would keep me from running out of fuel before the next exit, which was 11 miles ahead. Anxiously, I watched the gauge and soon found myself pulling into a gas station on the next exit. After I filled up with gas, I noticed a Kroger store a few blocks away and decided to pick up some "Little Debbie" snacks and a soft drink so I wouldn't have to stop again for lunch. En route to the store, I noticed a "used book and clothing" store just opposite one of the entrances. I felt a strong impression to go in. However, the last thing in the world I needed was more used books or clothing, so I headed to Kroger and got my snacks. As I left though, I again felt a very strong impression to go in.

As I walked in and looked around, I saw a G.E.D. study guide that would be useful the next time someone asked for help with their G.E.D. test. Then I saw a blue jean jacket that looked like it would fit one of my kids. The place had been quite busy when I entered it, but as I went to check out, I noticed it had emptied. I assumed that the store manager was who I was to witness to as he and a lady, whom I later learned was his wife, were the sole occupants in the store.

Not knowing how to start any meaningful conversation, I looked about for something to start talking about. As I paid for my items, my eye fell upon a nice collection of arrowheads in the glass case beneath the cash register.

Three hours later, I had shown him, his wife and young son, who later arrived from school, how Joseph had built the first pyramid, answered many questions they had about religion and was asking if it would be alright if I said a little prayer with them before I left. I prayed a simple, direct prayer for their health, happiness and especially for their salvation. Opening my eyes, I saw tears streaming down all three of their faces. The husband and father, in a trembling voice, explained how he had been in church all of his life, was an elder and greeted members at the door of his church, but until that day he hadn't really known that God and His salvation was a reality.

The joy of going on God's errands is addicting. If I have not experienced a "divine encounter" for more than a week, I go into a state of depression and prayerfully seek out what had made me useless to God and His work. He, in mercy, always makes me aware of the problem, helps me straighten it out and puts me back to work. Friends, don't settle for a pretended relationship with God! You can and must find the real thing!

One last experience I want to share. In August of 1978, my two sons and I had the thrill of a lifetime. After a brief research on the site at which the ancient Egyptian army drowned while pursuing Moses and the Habiru (slaves), we decided to go to Egypt and check it out. We found the site, and after a crash course in scuba diving, right before we left home we were able to photograph the remains of three chariots on the sea floor. We then hurried home, gathered some equipment that would enable us to bring some of these artifacts to the surface and went to Giza. There we met with and explained to Mr. Nassef Mohamed Hassan, the Director of Antiquities for the Giza/Saqqara District and who later became the Director of the Egyptian Department of Antiquities, how the pyramids were built and gave him a short paper with diagrams for the machines and methods. We left, Mr. Hassan happily studying our paper and us with our permission to retrieve some artifacts to bring to him for evaluation.

We headed back to the site and began diving. While I was swimming underwater at about a 30 foot depth, marking possible candidates for retrieval from among several skeletal and chariot remains, I got severely sunburned! I, foolishly, didn't realize this could happen, and my feet swelled to the point that I couldn't get into my diving equipment. We were devastated. There was nothing for us to do except travel to Jerusalem and wait for our A.P.E.X. flight home, nurse my burns and possibly return to Egypt and finish the project.

Arriving in Jerusalem, we settled into a very uncomfortable but very cheap youth hostel. We did some sight-seeing, read a lot and in general had a miserable time. One day, I decided to visit the Garden Tomb. That was to be a place and experience never to be forgotten.

Inside the shop, I visited with the people who ran it and shared the discovery of Noah's Ark, how Joseph built the pyramids and showed them the photographs of the chariot parts from the Red Sea crossing site. They in turn asked me to stay during the two and a half hour closing time from 12:00 noon until 2:30 p.m. and look the Garden Tomb area over for possible archaeological remains. Returning to the hostel, I told my boys of my plans, and they decided to stay there and read. So, I returned to the Garden Tomb.

While looking through the gift shop for some books, I noticed a red haired man that looked like he had helped hang his last friend. I spoke to him cheerfully, discovered him to be an American, chatted briefly, wished him a good day and walked into the garden area that was to close very shortly. I was examining a site where some ancient coins had been found when I became aware that someone was standing behind me. Turning around, I saw the red haired gentleman. He inquired as to what I was doing. After a brief explanation, he said, "You are a scientist; do you believe in God and the Bible?" Two and a half hours later, after answering his questions and showing him the answers in the Bible, I asked him if I could pray with him. He said, "yes," and when I opened my eyes, tears were just streaming down his face.

"God sent you to me." he said. He explained how he was a pastor and had been deeply and persistently impressed to come to Jerusalem and convert the Jews. He'd prayed for signs and gotten positive ones. He went on to explain that he had gotten the promise of the assistant pastorship at the only Baptist Church in Jerusalem but lost it when the previous one decided to stay at the last minute, after he and his family had sold their home and belongings and already arrived in Jerusalem. He told me how he had looked for work everywhere but could find none; how he'd borrowed money to send his family home. Just that morning, he'd gone to Haifa to ship their few personal belongings home and taken the bus back to Jerusalem. When he arrived back here, he said he'd felt a strong impression, which he was now inclined to ignore since his previous impressions had resulted in his situation, but nonetheless, he decided to walk the 42 blocks and had just arrived when I saw him in the gift shop. He'd asked the kind folks there if he could be allowed to stay there during the two and a half hour "closed" period, and they said o.k. Now, as the tears were still streaming, he said that now, for the first time in all his years as a minister, he had a saving message to preach.

I, in my disappointment at not being able to retrieve the chariot parts, asked him, "Why, since you are from Little Rock and I'm from Nashville, couldn't we have met maybe in Memphis or at least somewhere closer to home?"

"If you had known me before this experience, you would not have asked that question. I knew everything and wouldn't have listened to you or anyone else." was his reply.

Then, I shared with him my reason for being in the Middle East and my keen disappointment at not being able to complete what I had set out to do at the Red Sea. He then, assuming his role as a pastor and new friend, assured me that God had better plans than we had and would bring them about in good time. And if we were "teachable", he would use us. The Spirit moved greatly within the both of us, and at this, we both went our separate ways of service, rejoicing in our loving God.

When we experience the "divine encounters", we can be sure that those we witness to will ultimately be saved and, in most cases, become effective witnesses themselves, the thief on the cross being one of the few exceptions to this. But this is only possible if we allow God to use us in His work.

The unspeakable joy of knowing with certainty that you are where God wants you to be, doing exactly what He wants you to do, can be yours. And then, one day, the unspeakable joy of seeing your family and others you have helped lead to Christ, walking the streets of gold, eating of the tree of life and drinking from the river of life eternally, will also be yours.

THE WITNESSING PRAYER

I have shared with you my addiction to "divine appointments". God, in His mercy, has invited us sinners (in rehabilitation) to bear faithful witness to Him, His character and salvation. You, with me, can be certain that you are in His will by taking three simple steps:

1) Ask God, in Christ's name, to forgive and cleanse you of every sin that separates you from His will.

2) Pray the "witnessing prayer", that you may be honored of Him by being led by His Spirit to bear effective, saving witness and/or help someone for whom Christ died.

3) When He provides the "divine appointment", be totally honest and truthful whoever you witness to or help. There are a vast number out there who have and are bearing a false witness, but rationalize that they are doing God and mankind a service by "embellishing" the truth, making it more spectacular, "punching it up". The extreme end of allowing Satan to lead you in this falsification of the facts is to become a destroyer of yourself, your family and others. God cannot lie. When we do, even if we "do it for a good reason", we separate ourselves from the only saving source of power in the universe.

Effective "divine encounters" are reconfirmations from God that we are in His will. Attacks by Satan and his hosts, both human and demon, are another reconfirmation of our walk with God. No attacks means we're doing Satan's will, not God's.

Even Paul knew the real enemy for he said, *"Wherefore we would have come unto you, even I Paul, once and again; but Satan hindered us."* I Thessalonians 2:18. So friends, be aware. The Word of God is not an idle tale when we are warned, *"Be sober, be vigilant; because your adversary the devil, as a roaring lion, walketh about, seeking whom he may devour:"* I Peter 5:8. Don't believe those who tell you that if you are a true Christian, you won't have problems and everyone will love you. For that's a lie. Satan will disguise his evil and use as his agents those who are not Christians, though they may profess to be. *"Marvel not, my brethren, if the world hate you."* I John 3:13. But remember His promise, in the words of Christ Himself, *"And ye shall be hated of all men for my name's sake: but he that endureth to the end shall be saved."* Matthew 10:22.

Again, our choices are to either work for God, share and enjoy His salvation throughout eternity, or to fall into the grasp of a merciless demon, and share total and eternal destruction in the hell-fires which will destroy Satan and his evil angels; the same fire God uses to purify this world of the last vestiges of sin and sinners before He restores it to its Edenic beauty and makes it the eternal home of the *"nations of them which are saved . . ."* Revelation 21:24.

CHAPTER 11

UNDERSTANDING THE GEOLOGY OF THE EARTH AND THE FLOOD

To fully appreciate the cataclysmic nature of the Deluge, it is imperative that the reader have an understanding of the awe-inspiring geological forces involved in such a global upheaval.

PRE-FLOOD GEOLOGY

Equally important to the appreciation of the magnitude of geological change upon the planet is the need to reach a clear understanding of pre-flood geology. The history of the planet, in both sacred and secular writings, tells us of an earth, covered in water, achieving "dry land" only after considerable "divine" manipulation. It is difficult for me to accept the slaying of the "primeval dragon" by some ancient god as the source of land and people, which is the popular pagan explanation of our origin. However, as I review the creation narrative in Genesis, I am struck by the fact that it is the "laboratory notes" of the carefully observed "thawing of an ice planet".

"And the earth was without form and void; and darkness was upon the face of the deep." (Genesis 1:2.) A "water" planet, located in deep space, would be an ice planet. The extremely low temperature prevailing in space, unlighted by a sun-star, freezes all matter, even gases.

An early "entry" in the "lab report" of events states that, *"And the spirit of God moved upon the face of the waters."* (Genesis 1:2) To appreciate the effects of God hovering over a portion of an "ice-planet", a few characteristics of God's nature should be noted: *"For the Lord thy God is a consuming fire, . . ."* (Deuteronomy 4:24); *". . . the mountains flowed down at thy presence."* (Isaiah 64:3) This description informs us that God emits planet-altering heat energy.

In another "lab notation", we are told that the evening "darkness" and the morning "daylight" was the first day. The observer sees our "ice planet" approached by an intense heat source covering one side of the planet. It is then set in motion and begins to rotate against this heat source not unlike a beef on a barbecue spit. This records the initiation of the "earth day"; one rotation equals one day. Had the Spirit "moved" over the entire earth, there would have been "day" only.

The next entry reports the thawing and diffusion of the planet's frozen gases and the continued rotation of the planet against the heat source. *"And God said, Let there be a firmament in the midst of the waters, and let it divide the waters from the waters."* (Genesis 1:6) This records the thawing and nebulizing of the frozen gases and water, separating them from other thawing materials. They achieved a stasis, or equilibrium, between the vapor screen at the outer parameter of the gaseous atmosphere and the water on the earth's surface.

The observer records the next phase. The soil and other matter also begin to thaw, lessening the density of the planet and increasing its volume with the heat-produced expansion. These changes, occurring beneath a veneer of water in liquid state, would produce massive capillary action resulting in the surface waters being transported from the surface to aquifers (deep sub- terranean water pools) under the planet's surface; *". . . and let the dry land appear."* (Genesis 1:9.) Again we see the phrase, "and the evening and the morning" were the second and third days, as the planet's rotational motion continues. The ice planet has transformed into a planet with dry land and a gaseous atmosphere, all enclosed within a vapor screen. The fact that Moses, who wrote Genesis, or anyone else living prior to the 19th century, would have had absolutely no knowledge of the phases (steps) of the thawing of an "ice planet", proves the divine inspiration of the Genesis creation account.

We then note the igniting (setting fire) of the mass of combustible gases at the center of the solar system. *". . . Let there be lights in the firmament of the heaven to divide the day from the night; and let them be for signs and for seasons, and for days, and years:"* (Genesis 1:14) *"And God made two great day from the night; and let them be for signs and for seasons, and for days, and years:"* (Genesis 1:14) *"And God made two great lights; the greater light to rule the day, and the lesser light to rule the night: he made the stars also."* (Genesis 1:16.) Thus He created the sun, moon and the stars. The new heat source, the sun, replaces "the Spirit of God moving upon the face of the deep" as a greatly lessened by totally adequate source of heat and light. With this new heat source to "power" the moisture equilibrium and control light and darkness, a powerful God looks at His new "terrarium" and pronounces it "good". We are not told, in the Bible, when the sun, with its planets and their moons, was created. We are told that they were already in existence before the first day of the creation week, for only light was created the first day. *"And God said, Let there be light: . . .", "And the evening and the morning were the first day."* Genesis 1:3,5.

Some have held the view that all the stars in the universe were created on the fourth day of the creation week. That is impossible, because most of the stars we see are millions of light years away. The creation week was just approximately six thousand years ago. The fact that we now see the light from these stars proves that they were created millions of years ago. One argument against this is that God "created things full grown". If so, the light from these distant stars was created "full grown", already reaching earth upon their creation. Take note of the fact that as recently as two years ago, "novas" have been observed by our astronomers. This would not be possible if all the stars were lighted at the same time. The last nova observed left behind a set of planets (orbitals) when the flash of light faded. This is proof that novas are the light of God's creative work, not simply exploding suns as modern astronomy teaches. The mass of the sun was there, prior to the creation week, but as yet unlighted. When it was lighted, as recorded in Genesis 1:14-19, its light reflected off the planets and their moons, thus our sun, moon and stars became visible for the first time on the fourth day of creation week.

Vegetation is noted on the third day, fishes and fowls on the fifth, and the introduction of animals and human life on the sixth. God rests during the seventh rotation of the planet, having ended the thawing out, beautification and introduction of various life forms upon planet earth.

This produced a planet whose vapor screen was held aloft by the combined buoyancy produced by a carefully calculated rotational velocity and the warm air lift produced by the sun's heat. This heat was conserved within the planet's vapor screen. Earth possessed a "minerally" homogeneous, uniformly heated and watered environment in which the life forms grew to massive size and lived a great number of years (as illustrated by the massive skeletal remains of the pre-flood antecedents of present day life forms).

It is sufficient to say that the "Biblical lab report" successively relates the detailed steps of an ice planet's meltdown, whose mass was created at an undisclosed time "in the beginning". This was then transformed into a verdant terrarium by "divine" manipulation of its elements during six literal successive days. This process is accurately described by Moses in a "lab report" written no later than the 14th century B.C.E.

THE FLOOD

What forces acting upon the above-described planet could produce the sacred and secularly described "deluge"?

The answer is found in a careful evaluation of the several minerals whose crystals align themselves with the magnetic north during their formation; example, magnetite. These crystals show that our planet changed its alignment a minimum of six times in rapid succession. What would be the effect of such action upon the pre-flood earth? *"Which removeth the mountains, and they know not: which overturneth them in his anger. Which shaketh the earth out of her place, and the pillars thereof tremble." Job 9:6,7.*

The buoyancy necessary to support the vapor screen outside the atmosphere and the centrifugal force required to maintain the volume of the planet in a state of equilibrium, holding the aquifers in stasis, would be violently interrupted. The resulting cataclysmic contortion of the planet would precipitate the water in the vapor screen violently down upon the surface. At the same time, the contraction of the planet would spew the contents of the aquifers skyward with incredible force.

In Genesis 7:11-24 and 8:2, we read, *"In the six hundredth year of Noah's life, in the second month, the seventeenth day of the month, on that day all the fountains of the great deep were broken up, and the windows of heaven were opened. And the rain was on the earth forty days and forty nights. In the selfsame day entered Noah, and Shem, and Ham and Japheth, the sons of Noah, and Noah's wife, and the three wives of his sons with them, into the ark. They, and every beast after his kind, and all the cattle after their kind, and every creeping thing that creepeth upon the earth after his kind, and every fowl after his kind, every bird of every sort. And they went in unto Noah into the ark, two and two of all flesh, wherein is the breath of life. And they that went in, went in male and female of all flesh, as God had commanded him: and the Lord shut him in. And the flood was forty days upon the earth; and the waters increased, and bare up the ark, and it was lifted up above the earth. And the waters prevailed, and were increased greatly upon the earth; and the ark went upon the face of the waters. And the waters prevailed exceedingly upon the earth; and all the high hills, that were under the whole heaven, were covered. Fifteen cubits upward did the waters prevail; and the mountains were covered. And all flesh died that moved upon the earth, both of fowl, and of cattle, and of beast, and of every creeping thing that creepeth upon the earth, and every man: All in whose nostrils was the breath of life, of all that was in the dry land, died. And every living substance was destroyed which was upon the face of the ground, both man and cattle, and the creeping things, and the fowl of the heaven; and they were destroyed from the earth: and Noah only remained alive, and they that were with him in the ark. And the waters prevailed upon the earth an hundred and fifty days." "The fountains also of the deep and the windows of heaven were stopped, and the rain from heaven was restrained;"*

The violently plummeting waters from the vapor screen, in concert with the spewing forth of the subterranean waters, would tear at the earth's surface, resulting in a planet-wide sea of "earth soup". All of the elements down to the bedrock; all plant and animal life were awash in a suspension of mud and debris, stirred in a cauldron of the violently warring forces of nature.

The wind velocity, with resultant chill factor, achieved

as the earth shook *"out of her place"* (Job 9:7), can only be appreciated by a look at its results. The frozen carcasses of ancient mammoths found, still preserved, in Alaska and Siberia; the condition of their flesh shows that they were frozen quickly by temperatures approaching absolute zero. These massive carcasses, with green vegetation remains still in their mouths and stomachs, are still edible when found today.

The geological record of the planet shows irrefutably that most of its surface has been cloaked in massive, icy glaciers. Geologists have determined, by measuring the compression of the soil and the pressure of the glaciers' weight, reflected in the scarring of the bedrock over which they passed, that these glaciers exceeded one mile in depth. The waters of the flood were frozen by the same chilling action that froze the carcasses of the mammoths. There is no force of nature operating at present that could possibly freeze tons of flesh (the mammoths) in the short time required to leave them in the quick-frozen condition in which they are found.

The "flip-flopping" of the planet, proven by the multiple magnetic polar orientation lines in the magnetite, is the only possible explanation capable of producing the "tortured and frozen planet scenario" so eloquently portrayed in an honest review of the geology of the planet.

As we read the "observer's lab notes" in the book of Genesis, we find an eloquent, if not understated, report of the forces of nature, set on "maximum destruct", that so altered the surface of our planet that few traces of its original beauty have survived.

These actions resulted in the suspension of all the planet's soil, to the depth of the bedrock, and the freezing of the water covered planet, approximating its condition on the first day of the original thaw with the exception of an approximately 40 degree band on both sides of the equator. This produced the second, and last, ice-age, the first being the period between the creation of the solar system and the creation week described in Genesis, an undisclosed period of time.

There have been well documented cases where the

footprints of man and dinosaur appear side by side, being made at close to the same time. The best documentation comes from the dinosaur tracks in the Paluxy River in the Glen Rose region of Texas. Some "creationist" scientists have observed that the red tint that is common in and around dinosaur tracks is also present in these human footprints and therefore conclude that the human footprints are actually dinosaur prints. Do these people actually believe that the dinosaurs produce some sort of "ooze" that ran down to their feet that turned their prints this reddish tint? Since this tint is present in all depressions in the strata displaying the dinosaur prints, is not a better explanation that the growth of some pre-flood algae or other pigment-producing organism was present in the standing waters left in these depressions? Or perhaps that some chemical reaction or mineral deposits occurring during the flood left this reddish stain on many surviving pre-flood surface indentations?

These same scientists also fail to recognize the fact that pre-flood vegetation had no seasonal growth rings. One confirmation of the authenticity of the boat-shaped object in eastern Turkey being the actual remains of Noah's Ark is the absence of growth rings in the petrified timbers. These men, upon observance of the structural remains that appear at regular intervals, declared them to be rocks! Genesis 2:6 tells us plainly that there was no rain, that a mist went up and watered the whole face of the earth. Are not growth rings the result of a variance in water supply and seasonal temperature changes in trees and other vegetation?

POST-FLOOD GEOLOGY

While the earth was "shaken out of her place", with all her water on the surface, the hydraulic forces swept all of the soil, stones and minerals violently into a churning suspension. This seething, boiling suspension of stone, vegetation and now expired life forms ground deep into what was later to be classified as "pre-cambrian" bedrock, leaving massive pot holes and scars.

In areas distant from the equatorial belt, the bone-chilling temperature produced by the long absence from sunlight, coupled with the shrieking wind velocities reaching many miles per hour, quickly froze the waters with their burden of suspended flood debris.

The waters at first gouged and tore at the very foundations of the planet. Then, as velocity and direction of rotation slowed and varied, they laid down alternating layers of vegetation and earthen debris which became the massive coal beds and the "geological column" of post-flood earth. The torque exerted upon the planet wrinkled and distorted the surface, rending gaping abysses later to be the receptacles for the post-flood seas. Great wrinkles were produced that are the towering mountain chains of post-flood geology. The reality of these violent gyrations of the planet are chronicled in the multidirectional magnetic pole oriented crystals formed during this action, i.e. magnetite. As the hydraulic action slowed, the elements precipitated out of the solution (earth soup), began to "clump" and migrated downward in the order of their density. While the soil of pre-flood earth was homogeneous, the soil of post-flood earth was a conglomeration of clumped minerals, vegetation and dead life forms. This left the post-flood surface soil with mere traces of the nutrient elements that were so abundant in pre-flood soil.

The levels (strata) at which the mineral agglutination occurred was determined by their varying densities and saturation factors. The radio isotopic minerals sought the lowest stratigraphic level in the redispositioned flood debris. As these radio isotopic minerals approached critical mass in their clumping process, they generated intense heat, several times hotter than that of the sun. This process, enhanced by the confining over-burden of flood debris, resulted in the thermal vitrification of trillions of cubic yards of magma. As the elements achieved their thermal liquefaction temperature level, they expanded in response to the exponentially magnified molecular activity produced by the increased heat. This resulted in the upward expansion of the earth's crust, resulting in a massive fissurization of the crust.

Where the fissionable material was redeposited and

concentrated, greater temperature and volumes of vitrification were achieved. In many areas, the pressure reached levels that penetrated the overlying strata in fissure or puncture configuration, producing ribbon and/or columnar eruption (extrusion) of the magma producing volcanos.

Meanwhile, on the surface of the planet, the flood waters had frozen in place, leaving only a belt of unfrozen water confined to approximately 40 degrees of latitude on either side of the equator. A "great wind" dried up most of these waters leaving a dry land belt approximately six thousand feet below present sea level.

Beneath these twin hemispherical ice-caps, the boiling magma produced by the nuclear fission at the lowest level of the "flood-laid" strata of the earth's crust, seethed, parried and thrusted. As the extruding magma forced its way relentlessly outward through the succeeding layers of flood-deposited overburden, it melted its way through the mile thick mantle of ice. This continued activity produced massive inland, ice-bound, melt-water seas. When the earth slowed to a revolutionary speed, diminished by approximately one twenty fourth of its pre-flood velocity, the storm cloud/flood scenario dissipated, and the sun began once again to shine on the vastly altered surface of the earth. This sunshine provided the energy to power the post-flood weather cycle.

The waters in the lakes and streams of the equatorial region were evaporated into clouds, these clouds being swept bilaterally poleward. When the moisture-laden clouds swept over the mantles of hemispheric ice, they cooled, releasing their burden of moisture as snow and rain. This added unremitting weight to the glaciers. This accumulated weight exerted sufficient downward pressure to force the lateral equatorial extrusion of the ice sheets. An equilibrium was achieved. (WEIGHT OF SNOW AND ICE > RESISTANCE TO GLACIAL FLOW = GLACIER FLOW RATE)

The heat of the sun gradually melted the walls of ice faster than their extrusion rates, persistently melting the walls of ice poleward. The evaporated waters were free of flood debris, and as they displaced the frozen flood waters, which bore the remains of pre-flood animals and vegetation, these ice-born remains were slowly and imperceptibly carried toward the equator.

The flesh and bones of the animals and the fruits, grains, nuts and fiber of the pre-flood vegetation were unceremoniously deposited, along with immeasurable tons of silt, gravel and other flood debris, producing many feet in depth of glacially laid moraine.

THE DINOSAUR MYTH

Obviously, during the "flip-flopping" of the earth on its axis, the action of the waters and debris was much like placing a handful of dirt in a jar of water and shaking it up. The destruction upon the face of the earth was total and complete, with the exception of the Ark and those secured inside. The devastation was far beyond our imagination. The minerals were no longer equally distributed throughout the earth, for after the tremendous force of the pole reversals, the centrifugal force of the rotation of the earth caused them to separate according to their density. The initial forces not being equal in all areas resulted in the varying strata in the different geographical areas. The remains (bones, etc.) of the people and animals were cast about in every direction. Again, the degree of the cataclysmic forces varying in areas, the result was that today we find conglomerations of bones, none or few attached to each other, and in most cases, not even related to each other.

The myth of the dinosaur is the direct result of men finding these accumulations of various animal and human remains and "force-fitting" the bones to form what they perceive to be a pre-historic animal. Yes, the bones are huge, and the animals were gigantic by our standards, but they were just very large specimens of the same animals we have on earth today, with the exception of a few that have become extinct. Remember that when God created the earth, it was perfect. The soil was of a perfect mixture to provide perfect nutrition. Men, as evidenced in Genesis, lived to extreme longevity, and it follows that the animals would do the same. Geology books are full of examples; an 18 inch wingspan dragonfly; ground sloths of 15 to 18 foot length; armadillos up to 8 feet long. The so-called "dinosaurs" were in many cases reptiles, and it must be remembered that reptiles, unlike other animals, continue to grow as long as they live. If they lived 500, 600, perhaps even 800 or 900 years, it stands to reason that their size would be tremendous. It has been amply demonstrated by the endless string of "hoaxes" perpetrated by the collectors of "prehistoric skeletons" that many of these "skeletons" are more the product of a wild imagination than scientifically reassembled remains of actual creatures.

Even the plant life was gigantic. The "horsetail rush" reached heights of 60 to 90 feet with diameters of 1 or 2 feet. Club mosses attained 50 to 100 feet heights and had 2 to 4 foot diameters. Another note of interest is the fact that these pre-flood trees lack the growth rings that are present in post-flood plants.

Like the "clumping" of the minerals, the density of the animal debris played a part in its distribution on and in the earth as the catastrophic event came to a close. However, another factor contributed to this also: the reactions of the animal or human as the cataclysm began. Obviously, the sea animals had no choice but to remain in the water. The less mobile animals were restricted in the escape actions. The largest animals, no doubt due to their great size, were slow and incapable of seeking high ground as the flood waters rose. But the people obviously tried to get to the highest ground possible. The birds were disabled by the intense rain and wind. The result was that certain types of animal life were deposited earlier than others. Man, still obviously believing he could escape, went to the tops of the highest hills. Some probably tied themselves to giant trees. Ultimately, all flesh upon the face of the earth was destroyed and deposited in flood-laid strata in the order dictated by their density and mobility.

As the flood waters receded, bodies of man and animals

were lying everywhere in the inhabited areas. Then, the "great wind", which helped dry up the waters, moved even the earth with its great force. Trees, rocks and earth were heaped upon the bodies. When Noah finally looked outside and saw the land, it was totally barren of every living thing. The enormous forests were totally buried and are today the vast coal and oil fields.

UNDERSTANDING PETRIFICATION

A synopsis of the petrification (mineral replacement) process will help the reader understand what happened to pre-flood remains. The classical steps in petrification involve the "burying" of the object (wood, bone, etc.) beneath the soil. This is usually accomplished by the object being carried by wind or flood into an area where the water table lies near the surface. In some cases, massive mud flows pour into a low lying forest area, inundating the vegetation and maintaining a water level above the buried organic object.

The soluble minerals are dissolved in the water, then this heavily mineralized water is filtered through the organic object. As the object decays or dissolves away, the resulting empty spaces (voids) are filled as the mineralized water deposits its excess minerals when slowed by the filtering actions of the dissolving object. This process progresses at a rate determined by the availability of soluble minerals, water to dissolve and transport them and finally, the decay rate of the object being petrified. The Britannica states it thusly; "hard structure is dissolved and simultaneously replaced by another substance . . .". Therefore, it becomes obvious that petrification must closely pace the decay rate of the object being petrified, cell by cell, or the petrification process would be impossible. And as the decay rate of all organic materials is measured in days, months and years, not millions of years, it is obvious that petrification occurs far quicker than scientists would have us to believe. In "A Young People's Guide to the Bible and the Great Dinosaur

Mystery" by Paul S. Taylor, he states; *"Scientists have found that chicken bones and wood can be fossilized in just five to ten years. A big dinosaur bone might take hundreds of years to completely fossilize;"*.

It is important for us to have an understanding of this process to understand that the human skulls, represented by scientists as being millions of years old, can be perhaps only 100 years old. In Yuma, Arizona, a female prisoner at the Federal prison located there was buried in a nearby cemetery in the late 1800's. About 70 or 80 years later, a crew excavating the area in order to build the highway through there discovered her remains; she was completely petrified. Cell by cell, her body had been replaced by lime, and she is now referred to as the "Limestone Lady". Out of respect for the deceased, her body is not on display any longer.

POST-FLOOD: LIFE BEGINS AGAIN

Noah and his family, along with the animals, disembarked from their Ark and began to proliferate. Expanding geographically, the peoples were soon scattered around the dry land belt, separated by language groups after the Tower of Babel scenario. The original eight survivors of the flood were pre-flood people and of enormous stature. However, because of the loss of the perfect nutrition provided by the pre-flood soil and atmospheric conditions, man rapidly, from generation to generation, began to decrease in height. His life-span was also shortened as evidenced in Genesis chapter 11 and 50:26— from Shem's death at 602 years to Joseph's at 110 years shows a 545% decrease over 12 generations. The first three generations after Shem showed an approximate 25% decrease. The next three decreased approximated 33% from the prior three generations, and when we finally arrive at Joseph's 110 years, we find a 545% overall decrease from Shem. Of note is that Abraham and Isaac lived beyond the expected life-span for their generation, and this can be directly attributed to the fact that they complied with the "clean/unclean" diet specifications dictated by God. The Hebrew word translated "unclean", used in the scriptures relating to animals, means defiled or polluted. Obviously, God gave these restrictions because these animals were not healthy for man to eat, and by adhering to His statutes, Abraham and Isaac were far healthier than those who consumed the "unclean" animals. This phenomena is still recognized in the longevity of the people of Hunza, Georgia, USSR and certain tribes in New Guinea. It has only been in our recent past that we have learned to produce vitamin supplements and measure the nutritional values in our foods thus enabling us to provide better nutrition for ourselves. And in 1900, the average life expectancy at birth for a male was 47.9 years and 51.1 years for a female. With our increased knowledge of nutrition, by 1975 these figures had risen to 69.5 years for males and 75.8 for females.

The size or stature of man rapidly decreased after the flood also due to the nutritional factor. Again, both in Britain and the U.S., statistics show that from a little prior to 1900 until today children under average economic conditions have increased in height at age 10 to 14 years by .08 to 1.2 inches per decade for an average total of nine inches through our present decade. While a portion of this figure reflects an earlier maturation, it also reflects a significant increase in height since full maturity (height) is attained shortly after this age. Though many argue that heredity plays a large part in height and size, it must be remembered that the complex system that regulates the human growth factor, ultimately, no matter what genetic material or DNA is available, must be well nourished to function properly.

WERE THERE REALLY POST-FLOOD GIANTS?

As Noah's descendants proliferated and filled the confining boundary of the ice-enclosed, post-flood, dry land belt, those living near the extruding glaciers soon became aware of the availability of pre-flood foodstuff preserved in the melting face of the ice. The "quick-frozen" mammoths, as one example, provided more than adequate supplies of food while eliminating the necessity of hunting and killing animals. The carcasses left behind, coupled with the absence of weaponry capable of killing such monstrous beasts, created a quandary for post-flood paleontologists and geologists who were unfamiliar with or flatly refused to accept the flood scenario. However, there was a very important "side-effect" that accompanied the eating of the pre-flood foodstuffs; these foodstuffs were composed of the perfect nutrition in existence prior to the flood; the peoples living in this belt, receiving the perfect nutrition of the pre-flood substances, grew larger, or at least retained their pre-flood size. In referring to a world map, it is noted that the 40 degree mark on the northern hemisphere runs directly through the area of the mountains of Ararat. The giants spoken of in the Bible were the direct descendants of these peoples, who remained near the outer belt for many years. Today, in Dogubeyazit, Turkey, are to be found numerous skeletal remains of these giants, one example I have personally seen and photographed, being human jaw bones of such size as to fit easily over the jaw of the largest man today. The disappearance of these giants from the Biblical record as quickly as they appeared is directly attributed to the fact that as soon as they were deprived of their pre-flood food substance, they succumbed to the diminished stature resulting from post-flood nutrition. This could have been accomplished in one generation but most probably not beyond two at the most.

THE ICE AGE ENDS

As the earth settled and the glaciers began to melt, the ever-rising water level in the dry-land belt produced seas, lakes and rivers whose fish-bearing, commercial waters attracted to their shores the centers of early ziggurat/ pyramid civilizations.

As the fires beneath the earth continuously produced the surface-seeking magma, the melt-water, inland seas increased progressively and geometrically in size and weight. As the walls of ice separating these seas from the low land of the equatorial belt thinned, a point was reached where these walls could no longer contain the surging tides of the inland seas. As these walls ruptured, the waters and "slime" of the inland seas spewed forth, ponderously and irresistibly invading and inundating the low-lying centers of the early civilizations.

In a day and a night, these waters engulfed ancient Atlantis, Mu and other legendary civilizations of antiquity. The remains of these ancient civilizations, found 6,000 feet below present sea-level, are the puzzling "heralds", along with Plato's account of the inundation of Atlantis, of the emptying of the massive inland seas into the low-lying, equatorial, dry-land belt.

During the 4,000 plus years of post-flood history, the melt-back, the resupplied rain cycle and the extrusion of the planet's glaciers has reached near equilibrium. The recent diminishing of the ozone layers above the earth's atmosphere has triggered a resurgence of glacial melt. During this same period of time, the clumping tendency of the fissionable elements in the earth's crust has produced a volatile geological state for this planet.

"But the day of the Lord will come as a thief in the night; in the which the heavens shall pass away with a great noise, and the elements shall melt with fervent heat, the earth also and the works that are therein shall be burned up." II Peter 3:10.

Isaiah 9:5 tells us of the *"confused noise"* and of *"garments rolled in blood"* with *"burning and fuel of fire"*. Psalms 11:6 tells us God will rain *"snares, fire and brimstone, and a horrible tempest: (and burning wind)"*. As the waters from heaven united with the waters gushing from the earth to destroy the wicked during the flood, could it be that the depths of the earth contain the arsenal by which the Lord will destroy the wicked this time? *"But the heavens and the earth, which are now, by the same word are kept in store, reserved unto fire against the day of judgment and perdition (destruction) of ungodly men."* II Peter 3:7.

CHAPTER 12

WHY ARE THESE THINGS BEING PRESENTED TO THE WORLD NOW?

As evidenced throughout the Bible, God presents different truths to His people at different times depending on our needs. Unfortunately for most of us, we are not aware of how badly we are in need of a true connection with our Lord, of a daily living experience with Him.

We have no way of comparing our present spiritual situation with that of the peoples of past history except by a study of the history of our world and to read and know the Bible. Many of us suffer from the delusion that we are doing great compared to those around us. Satan has really pulled the wool over our eyes as to the real truth, for like Solomon, our apostasy has been gradual. The insidious poison of evil has blinded us.

"For we dare not make ourselves of the number, or compare ourselves with some that commend themselves: but they measuring themselves by themselves, and comparing themselves among themselves, are not wise." II Corinthians 10:12.

All through history, the true Christians were persecuted, tortured and even martyred because of their faith. The hatred that led to Christ's crucifixion would continue to burn in the heart of the world against all who were His followers. Beginning with Nero, Christians were accused of horrible crimes. Some were then crucified, some were ripped apart by wild animals in arenas, and thousands were burned alive while tied atop tall poles in Nero's courtyard.

For hundreds of years Christians were pursued as beasts of prey and had to hide. Yet in spite of this, Christianity flourished. Realizing that he couldn't victor over Christ by the killing of the body, Satan implemented a new plan.

In 313 A.D., Constantine decreed Christianity to be the official religion of the empire. While the persecutions ceased, this set the stage for the deterioration of the church. At this time, most of the people were heathens, and in order to make Christianity appealing to the heathens, their practices were incorporated into the church. They had their priests, altars and sacrifices, and soon so did the church. Their superstitions and magical objects were transformed into the veneration of the relics of the martyrs and saints. Christianity was nothing more than a new name for their heathen worship. The worst part was that it became difficult for the true Christian to see the truth through the deceptions.

Before long, the church began to persecute the heretics and "heathens." Once again, the true Christians faced persecution. And throughout the ages until our present day, the church has deteriorated through Satan's devices.

Paul tells us that *"all that will live godly in Christ Jesus shall suffer persecution."* II Timothy 3:12. As long as there was persecution, the church remained relatively steadfast and pure. But the church as a whole today is so tainted as to be virtually devoid of true religion. The great struggle now is not to escape death or martyrdom as a result of our faith, but to see the truth through the deceptions. Paul saw these things creeping into the church even in his day as he wrote, *"the mystery of iniquity doth already work."* II Thessalonians 2:7.

The early history of our country reveals how vital our forefathers' dependence on God was. When man has nothing, when he has to till the soil and live off the fruits of his own labor, if he has faith in God, he can see His power in his daily life. But as we progressed, an evil pattern began to emerge.

As power struggles develop and men discover that through their power they can benefit from the labors of others, the time inevitably comes that a choice must be made. These men must choose between God and their own devices. As they decide, greed, love of pleasure and ease step in. Satan whispers in their ear that God only forbids things because He knows you can be like Him, that He wants to keep you in ignorance, the same lie he deceived Eve with. The same lie of the "new age" movement - that we can "tap in" to God's wisdom because after all, we're all a part of Him and therefore, are Him. An easy pill to swallow for those looking for a way out.

But look at slavery of our own not-too-distant past. Man soon learns to rationalize his every action against the inner-promptings which tell him right from wrong. Like a callous which forms from repeated abuse, the heart becomes hardened, at first unwilling and finally unable to hear and accept the truth.

"Thy princes are rebellious, and companions of thieves: everyone loveth gifts and followeth after rewards: they judge not the fatherless, neither does the cause of the widow come unto them." Isaiah 1:23.

For just a moment, let's look at our country today. We've legalized abortions so we can pursue our sexual pleasures without suffering the burdens. *"Ah sinful nation, a people laden with iniquity, a seed of evildoers, children that are corrupters: they have forsaken the Lord, they have provoked the Holy One of Israel unto anger, they are gone away backward."* Isaiah 1:4.

Our legal system is a mockery of justice; with a good lawyer who can find the "loop-hole", murderers and rapists go free, yet a woman who hides her young daughter from the child's sexually-abusive father sits in jail for almost two years with no relief in sight. *"Woe unto them that call evil good and good evil; that put darkness for light, and light for darkness; that put bitter for sweet, and sweet for bitter!"* Isaiah 5:20.

We have the finest hospitals in the world, and the Lord has imparted great knowledge of healing to our men of medicine. And as long as we have enough insurance, we have access to these institutions, but if we are poor, we are turned away. *"For the poor shall never cease out of the land: therefore I command thee, saying, Thou shalt open thine hand wide unto thy brother, to thy poor, and to thy needy, in thy land."* Deuteronomy 15:11.

Taxed, as a means to run our great country efficiently, we are able to "shelter" our income and therefore pay little taxes if we are wealthy. If we are poor or even middle-classed, we are allowed few deductions and end up paying a much larger percentage of our income. If we don't have the money to pay our taxes, much less afford a high-priced tax attorney, we are at the total mercy of the tax-collectors. Without regard to families' needs, they have the power to garnish a person's wages, allowing him to keep only $75.00 per week. They can take our home and sell it for whatever price they choose, even if it is far below the market value. *". . . the spoil of the poor is in your houses. What mean ye that ye beat the faces of the poor? saith the Lord God of hosts."* Isaiah 3:14,15.

Our country was founded on the basis of freedom. Freedom of religion, freedom of speech, etc. We fought long and hard for the freedom of pornography and we got it, along with the deadly cesspool it creates. *"For as he thinketh in his heart, so is he."* Proverbs 23:7.

Because of television, our children grow up believing not only that adultery is acceptable, but that men who murder people left and right in Satan's "redesigned good victoring over evil" are heroes. *"Woe unto them that call evil good, and good evil; that put darkness for light, and light for darkness; that put bitter for sweet, and sweet for bitter!"* Isaiah 5:20.

Finally, we must look at our churches. God's house. We array ourselves in our finest attire and jewelry every Sunday, go and sit through a sermon while secretly hoping it's over soon so we can go play golf or watch the t.v. If we tithe at all, it's mainly for the tax write-off. We listen to the sermon in the air-conditioned comfort of our new $250,000.00 addition preached by a minister in a $300.00 suit who drives a Seville and will later go home to his 3,000 square-foot home. At the same time, on the other side of town, people are hungry, needing clothing and medical help. *"And Jesus saith unto him, The foxes have holes, and the birds of the air have nests; but the Son of God hath not where to lay His head."*

By now, I'm sure some of you are beginning to get defensive, saying "I'm certainly not like that" or "who are you to be saying all that?" But we must awaken to the truth of our situation. We cannot allow Satan to continue to deceive us and drag us down to his wretched depths. We are each and every one in grave danger unless we cling desperately to the Word of God.

There can be no doubt that Christ will soon return for His children. I cannot present the evidences God has preserved for us in these last days without presenting them for what they are - a chance for us to see the absolute truth as recorded in the Bible and evidences of God's past judgments.

Paul said *"Moreover, brethren, I would not that ye should be ignorant, how that all our fathers were under the cloud, and passed through the sea; And were baptized unto Moses in the cloud and in the sea."* Corinthians 10:1,2.

Timothy wrote for us the following warning, given by the Holy Spirit, that we would be aware of the seriousness and dangers we'd face: *"Now the Spirit speaketh expressly, that in the latter times some shall depart from the faith, giving heed to seducing spirits, and doctrines of devils; Speaking lies in hypocrisy;"* I Timothy 4:1. *"This know also, that in the last days perilous times shall come. For men shall be lovers of their own selves, covetous, boasters, proud, blasphemers, disobedient to parents, unthankful, unholy, Without natural affection, trucebreakers, false accusers, incontinent, fierce, despisers of those that are good, Traitors, heady, highminded, lovers of pleasure more than lovers of God; Having a form of godliness, but denying the power thereof: from such turn away."* II Timothy 3:1. We are told in no uncertain terms to "preach the Word", *"For the time will come when they will not endure sound doctrine; but after their own lusts shall they heap to themselves teachers, having itching ears; And they shall turn away their ears from the truth and shall be turned unto fables."* II Timothy 4:2-4.

We would have to be blind not to see that the days of which are written here are the days we are living in. While Thomas didn't believe until he could see in His hands the print of the nails, Christ offered him this evidence. He didn't condemn Thomas because he didn't believe until he saw, for He said, *"Reach hither thy finger, and behold My hands; and reach hither thy hand and thrust it into My side: and be not faithless, but believing. And Thomas answered and said unto Him, My Lord and my God. Jesus saith unto him, Thomas, because thou hast seen Me, thou hast believed: blessed are they that have not seen, and yet have believed."* John 20:27-29.

God desires that all men be saved. All through the Bible, we read of the mighty works of His Hand; how He gave

His children all the evidence we could imagine, that they should believe. Now He is preparing the way for new evidences, preserved by Him thousands of years ago for revealing in His time. Only today do we need "proof" that Noah really survived the flood. Only today do we find it impossible to believe God parted the Red Sea so Moses and the Israelites could cross on dry land. *"Beware lest any man spoil you through philosophy and vain deceit, after the tradition of men, after the rudiments of the world, and not after Christ."* Colossians 2:8.

Is this world really ready for Christ's return? Revelation describes the terrible condition of the religious world right before the end. And Revelation 12:12 tells us how Satan is going to have great wrath *"because he knoweth that he hath but a short time."* If this is the time of the end, we cannot deny the terrible state of the world. If we can't see it, it's because Satan has blinded us. But, *". . . As I live, saith the Lord God, I have no pleasure in the death of the wicked; but that the wicked turn from his way and live."* Ezekiel 33:11. *"And it shall come to pass in the last days, saith God, I will pour out of My Spirit upon all flesh:"* Acts 2:17. God is going to bring this world to a close with a tremendous show of His power. Right before the end, Revelation 18:1 states *"And after these things I saw another angel come down from heaven, having great power; and the earth was lightened with his glory."* Then this angel cries out to us, *"Babylon the great is fallen, is fallen, and is become the habitation of devils and the hold of every foul spirit, and a cage of every unclean and hateful bird."*

He's giving you proof that His judgments are real; that His Word is divinely inspired and accurate right down to every "jot and tittle". It's going to be up to you to accept the truth in your heart or reject it and listen to men who, as agents of Satan, will try to discredit God's work.

"And, behold, I come quickly; and my reward is with me, to give to every man according as his work shall be."

"I am Alpha and Omega, the beginning and the end, the first and the last."

"I Jesus have sent mine angel to testify unto you these things in the churches. I am the root and the offspring of David, and the bright and morning star." Revelation. 22:12,13,16

CONCLUSION

These great discoveries belong to you, the people of God's world. They are His gifts to His sinful children, an act of mercy that all those who <u>want</u> to know the Truth, will have a reason to believe. The arguments against the validity of the Scriptures go back as far as recorded history, for Satan knew from the beginning that he had to destroy God's Word in order to destroy His children.

Again, I cannot tell anyone why the Lord chose me. Perhaps it is because I was the only one who "volunteered"! I only followed as and where He led and can only give Him the credit.

I believe strongly that the time is close at hand when the Lord is going to complete these projects. As He leads, we will fully document everything and make it available to everyone.

We are presently finishing the full-sized book on Noah's Ark, complete with all the details of the search and final verification. Of course, the most conclusive evidence can only be obtained by excavation, so we ask that you pray that this will be allowed to take place.

We will have videos, both Christian version and scientific version, in the near future, on Noah's Ark.

The other projects are still in God's hands, but we are working steadily on them all. We plan to publish a series of books that will give the details of the many objects and sites of our research. Here is a list of their titles:

1. DISCOVERED: NOAH'S ARK.

2. DISCOVERED: HOW AND WHO BUILT THE PYRAMIDS.

3. DISCOVERED: ROUTE AND RELICS OF 1446 B.C. EXODUS.

4. DISCOVERED: GIANTS!

5. DISCOVERED: ARK OF THE COVENANT!

6. DISCOVERED: DIARY OF PLANET EARTH.

7. DISCOVERED: DIARY OF THE DEMON.

8. REDISCOVERED: GOD.

These books will contain the research on many and varied objects, locations, and significances of 40 years research that have proven to your highly skeptical writer the realities of God and satan, and how we can cooperate with God, successfully resist satan and gain eternal life.

NOAH'S ARK TOUR INFORMATION

A great number of people have expressed an interest in going to Turkey and visiting the Ark. We have discussed this matter with Dr. Nathan Meyer, Evangelist and Bible Teacher, who has taken over 60 tour groups to Israel, and who has visited the Ark himself. He has agreed to explore this possibility with us, so if you think you might be interested in such a trip, please write to his office and tell them you may be interested. If enough people express interest, we will put together such a tour and send you the information as it becomes available.

Please write to:

BIBLE PROPHECY ASSOCIATION
BOX 442
WORTHINGTON, OHIO 43085